CALAMITY JANE, SCOUT, FREIGHTER AND
FRONTIERSWOMAN

(From a photograph taken in 1876, found under an old building.)

Old Deadwood Days

By
Estelline Bennett

University of Nebraska Press
Lincoln & London

Reprinted from the original edition of 1928
Manufactured in the United States of America

First Bison Book printing: 1982

Most recent printing indicated by the first digit below:
7   8   9   10

Library of Congress Cataloging in Publication Data

Bennett, Estelline.
  Old Deadwood days.

  Reprint. Originally published: New York: J. H. Sears, c1928.
  1. Deadwood (S.D.)—History. 2. Frontier and pioneer life—
South Dakota—Deadwood. I. Title.
F659.D2B4   1982   978.3'91   81–14737
ISBN 0–8032–1173–2   AACR2
ISBN 0–8032–6065–2 (pbk.)

∞

Dedicated to

The Memory of

My Father

CHARACTERS

In the pages of this book these famous frontier characters play their several parts in the drama of American civilization's Western march.

DEADWOOD DICK . . .	"In person"—as he really was
CALAMITY JANE . . .	A Helen of Deadwood, so to speak
WILD BILL HICKOK . .	Prince of Pistoleers, who died by one
MADAME CANUTSON .	A prima donna of bull-whackers
SETH BULLOCK . . .	Roosevelt's sheriff friend
JUDGE BENNETT . . .	Who brought law to Deadwood
PREACHER SMITH . .	A sky pilot without a compass
BELLE HASKELL . . .	The best known Madame in town
AL SWEARENGER . . .	Proprietor of the Gem Theater
BLONDE MAY ⎱ . . . ⎰ KITTY ARNOLD	Calamity Jane's protégées of joy
COLORADO CHARLIE . .	A fisher for gold
MIKE RUSSELL . . .	A good saloon keeper
BUCKSHOT BILL . . .	A "Casey Jones" of the hills
MABEL FENTON . . .	Another of the girls
SCOTT DAVIS	A shotgun messenger
COLD DECK JOHNNY .	A knight of the stud table
SLIPPERY SAM	Should have been an eel
CROW DOG	Just an Indian
MINERAL JACK . .	A searcher for the Golden Fleece
CALIFORNIA JACK . .	Master of the faro box
GENERAL DAWSON . .	The author's avuncular guide
SWILL BARREL JIMMY .	A derelict

THE ILLUSTRATIONS IN THIS BOOK

It is deplorable that science has not yet perfected a camera capable of photographing the scenes and personages of a day that has gone. Otherwise the present note on the illustrations in this volume would be superfluous. Dim they may be, in many instances, the pictures in the book, but one must recall that, taken back in the gaudy days of Deadwood's greatest glory, the original photographs have lain for all these years, until unearthed by the author of the work, in bedraggled and threadbare albums, in ancient and forgotten trunks, and in dusty attic corners. None the less, they do enhance the value of Miss Bennett's book, which will be accepted by the student of Western development, no less than by the reader seeking entertainment only, we believe, as a definite addition to Americana.

THE PUBLISHERS

CONTENTS

LIST OF ILLUSTRATIONS

A Little Girl In Old Deadwood

Chapter 1

A LITTLE GIRL IN OLD DEADWOOD

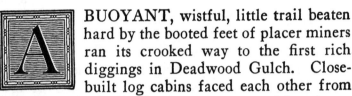 BUOYANT, wistful, little trail beaten hard by the booted feet of placer miners ran its crooked way to the first rich diggings in Deadwood Gulch. Close-built log cabins faced each other from behind pathetically important square false fronts across a rough road in the building of a Main street never intended for permanence. Ten thousand venturesome, excited gold seekers panned gold in the streams and crowded into the cabins in spite of orders from the United States Government to stay out of the Sioux reservation, and thus the outlaw camp of Deadwood was born. On the west, Forest Hill rose high and heavily timbered. On the east, White Rocks lifted their glittering limestone peak far above the noisy disorder of the young camp. Against every horizon mountains stood high and dark, in serene tolerance of the tumult at their feet.

The Government had recognized Deadwood's right to live and dig for gold by the time I set my sturdy little shoes on the board sidewalks of Sherman street to go to school in what was called "an old store building." I could not have been more than five years old. So, in a manner of speaking, Deadwood and I grew up together through stagecoach

and school days until the railroad came in and I
cried my way east to boarding school.

Of all the mining camps of the frontier, Deadwood flared highest and brightest. In one year it
wrote a noisy, bloody page of history that traveled
all over the world in a Wild West stagecoach and
between the covers of dime novels. It was young
longer than any town that ever grew and prospered
because it was off the railroad longer. For nearly
fifteen years it was a stagecoach town and then one
cold December morning the railroad came and in
that one day the merry young mining camp bloomed
into a surprised town with civic and moral obligations. It took it a long time to adjust itself and the
twentieth century dawned to find it still youthful and
still a little puzzled about its responsibilities.

Buffalo Bill, when he came into Deadwood on a
railroad train for the first time, told me he was not
surprised at the changes he found because railroads
always aged a town. "A town is young," he said,
"just as long as it stays off the railroad."

"It's too bad the railroad came," I commented.

"Oh, no," he said quietly but decidedly, "a town
is like a baby. It either grows up or dies." And
then he added with the ready optimism of the real
Westerner, "But Deadwood, you know, was young
so long it never will quite forget its youth."

There still is a wicked little fling to the very name.
It carries a thrill of adventure even after all these
years. A charmed something hung over the bright
clean young fortunes that were made overnight with
no capital but a pick, a shovel, and a gold pan. It
flung itself into the days when gold was uncovered

A Little Girl in Old Deadwood

in wide, deep veins of ore, and stamp mills roared through the gulches. There never was but one Deadwood.

Law and order came early in '77 and for more than a dozen years lawlessness and law, order and disorder drifted along together in the seclusion of the deep, narrow gulch without interfering seriously with each other. They emphasized the natural sharp contrasts of the camp in Deadwood Gulch.

Everything was in dramatic contrast except material prosperity. There were no destitute poor. The richest among us had made their money in mines and that was something everybody else expected to do to-morrow. Or their rich ore veins might fault or pinch out any day. Wealth dug out of gold mines created no class distinctions. In everything else the contrasts were sharp and clear. Days were divided into high noons and sudden nights. There were no golden pink dawns and no purple twilights. Winter mornings were dark until the high sun leaped, fully day-blown, from behind White Rocks, and then it was nearly noon. Sometimes it found clouds floating around in its way below White Rocks and put them summarily to rout. Somewhere in the middle of the afternoon before any sunset colors had time to assemble themselves, it dropped behind the pines on Forest Hill and day was gone. The seasons came in with a bang, and there you were. Only autumn slipped in gently at the end of a summer of bright days and crisp, cool nights and an occasional flurry of snow, trailing its purple veils over the gorgeousness of scarlet sumach, golden aspen, and scrub oak.

Deadwood was a wide-open town in the 'eighties

Old Deadwood Days

with saloons and gambling houses and painted ladies
—its spectacular vices on parade for all the world to
see. But the homes on Forest Hill's one-sided streets
and in the secluded hollow of Ingleside were as
sheltered as the courtyard of a convent. What
growing up Deadwood saw of the other side of life
merely was a bit of highly colored drama that we
didn't understand. We lived our lives in our homes,
in school, Sunday school, church, and among the
pines, rocks, and wild flowers on the mountains that
rose high above the houselines of the town, shutting
us in, together with the "badlands," away from the
rest of the world—so far away.

The lovely light ladies—pretty, beautifully
gowned, and demure mannered—were, many of
them, known by face and name to everybody. But
their little span of glory was too brief to leave any
illusion in our minds about the desirability of such
lives. They collected their wages of sin under our
very eyes. We saw them on the street, in the stores,
at the theater on the rare occasions when there was
a play at Nye's Opera House or Keimer Hall. And
then, two or three years later, we saw these same
girls pallid and shabby, with dingy old "fascinators"
over their heads, slipping furtively down the alley
that ran back of Main street, in quest of the price
of a drink or a shot of dope. In a pathetically little
while they disappeared. Once in a long time one of
them married and escaped this fate. Some of them
avoided it by the route of poison or the little gun.
Without anyone calling our attention to it, we accepted the drab skulking procession as the inevitable
end of the easiest way.

6

A Little Girl in Old Deadwood

Along in that dim alley parade went "Swill Barrel Jimmy," in his long frock coat turning all the sad apologetic shades of purple and blue and green when it should have been black. His trousers were frayed and fringy around his ankles. His derby matched his coat in color, and his hair hung in long messy strings over the clean white collar he always wore. He lived on the extravagant wastefulness of the Chinese restaurants, saloons, and houses of low morals and high charity. He slept where he could. On cold nights he availed himself of the cordial, unquestioning hospitality of the well-warmed saloons. He never was known to speak to anyone except the clerks from whom he bought his white collars and he made these purchases with as few words as possible. His gratitude to the saloon men who gave him shelter was expressed in a courteous monosyllable. No one knew of a certainty anything about him, but it was said that he came from a good old Southern family, had been an officer in the Confederate army, and at the close of the Civil War had wandered heartbroken into the West.

Everything about those alleyways was of deep interest. They were the arteries of a strange, different life. I knew very well that what we saw was the least of the difference. There was one elderly *grande dame* in Deadwood in those days, probably in her fifties, seeming older to us because old age was something of which the children of Deadwood knew nothing. It was something they never saw. For the town was young and its men and women were young. Only youth could hazard the hard journey across the plains from the railroads to the Hills.

Old Deadwood Days

Only youth could make itself a part of the town that Deadwood was in the 'eighties. This woman whose hair was beginning to turn gray and who had not danced since she donned her long, heavy, black veil when her husband died years before, was so venerable and so much the aristocrat that she could do as she pleased and go where she liked. The use she made of her privileges made me regret my own sheltered youth, for she made friends with the ladies of the badlands. She visited with them in their parlors where they raised the curtains just a little to let in a bit of afternoon sun in her honor. She never intimated in manner or conversation that she recognized any difference between their way of life and her own. She said she found them gay and companionable. They would laugh and talk together for a little while just as though she were calling on a new mining man's wife and then she would make her *adieux* politely and go home. But three times during the years she lived in Deadwood, girls whom she knew in this way came to her house on Ingleside and asked her to help them get away into something different. She did this as blithely and casually as she had paid her visits. I heard her tell my mother once, sitting in our quiet front parlor with its square piano, its books and pictures and warm, red carpet, that of course that was the reason she had gone and the three girls had more than repaid her for any trouble—if it had been a trouble which she said it had not.

There was Nelly, she said, who always was rather a pitiful little figure, never quite adapted to the life. She was in Belle Haskell's house. Belle had been

A Little Girl in Old Deadwood

very kind in helping. She said some girls never could make good prostitutes——

Just then they discovered me sitting obscurely in my little rocking-chair intently reading Longfellow's poems, and Mother told me to go out and find Robbie and Gaylord. She hadn't heard their voices for some time and she didn't want them to wander too far from home. I obeyed very sadly and slowly.

I herded my little brothers home and then walked down the street to meet Father and the General coming home to dinner. They might have something interesting to tell and make me forget my disappointment over the unfinished story of Nelly.

Two men never were more unlike than my father and my mother's brother—the General—who made his home with us. Father was over six feet tall with black hair and mustache, dignified, and a little stern of aspect. General Dawson was a sandy blond with a long beard and his hat set rakishly at an angle. They came into the Hills a year apart, each in his own characteristic time. Father arrived in the spring of '77 after the treaty with the Sioux had been ratified. He came with an appointment from the President as Federal Judge with jurisdiction over all the Hills country.

He brought his family in the earliest 'eighties when the long stagecoach trail from the railroad was safe, and the little town in the gulch was comfortable. My own memory of the ride is that it was a delightful adventure. I think my mother disagreed with me. A stagecoach was a tireless thing. From the time it started on its journey, it never stopped until the end except to change horses and let us eat a little if we could get it. It rattled and rumbled and lurched all night as well as all day and you slept between the times you bumped your head against the side of the coach or fell off the seat. The water along the way was so bad that we carried with us bottles of cold tea—a most uninteresting drink. The most thrilling event of the night was the arrival at the stage station and the changing of horses. As we approached, the driver sent forth a clear, loud, "Yip-yip-yip, yi-yi-yi-yi," to waken the stock tender who had the fresh horses harnessed and waiting. We could hear their voices outside and through the narrow openings around the canvas curtains of the coach, we could see the lanterns and the shadows and dark bulks of the men and horses. Then the driver climbed to his high seat and everything was quiet except for the beat of the sixteen hoofs, and the dull thud of chunks of gumbo falling from the wheels. Sometimes it rolled up faster than it fell and then the driver, the messenger, and all the men passengers got down and scraped it off with spades carried for the purpose. Once when we were going into the Hills, the roads were so bad that we were delayed for days and we came to one dinner station where supplies had been delayed still longer and there was no food at all but beans—no bread, tea, coffee, or even salt. The wife of that stock tender was very unhappy about offering us such fare— utterly unadorned beans. But Mother, wise in the ways of traveling with little children, was carrying a lunch, and she shared her bread and salt with the stock tender's wife. When we came to places where

A Little Girl in Old Deadwood

they had dried-apple pie, we feasted regally. Once in the dark of the night we forded the Cheyenne River. The horses made a terrific commotion getting down the bank, and then the water splashed against us until we thought the whole river was coming in through the canvas flaps in a mad fury. Again, on the way, we met some men going out who had two small mountain lion cubs in a wooden crate. Sometimes we saw deer and small herds of antelope. On one occasion, I remember, we saw a lovely purple mass against the horizon that looked like turreted castles in a beautiful mountain range, and Father said it was a mirage. Two days later I called his attention again to a ragged purple mass against the sky. "Another mirage," I exclaimed excitedly. He smiled and shook his head. "No, not exactly," he said. "Those are the Black Hills."

The General came to the Hills with the outlaws of '76. That wild young year and the Civil War through which he rose to the rank of general, were the high lights in his life. To Father the war had been an unpleasant bloody incident, his service an accepted duty. He had been far more interested in the peaceful building of a state.

The General's stories of those days of '76 were of unfailing interest, especially that of the centennial Fourth of July celebration. Here was a little band of outlaws on ground that belonged to wards of the nation, flying the flag, firing salutes, and singing national airs with enthusiastic patriotism. It was the General who read the Declaration of Independence and it was he who drafted the memorial to Congress that was read and signed that day petitioning that "honorable body for speedy and prompt action in extinguishing the Indian title to, and opening for settlement the country we are now occupying and improving." Further it earnestly requested "that the government, for which we have offered our lives, at once extend a protecting arm and take us under its care."

It is a tribute to the General that, in spite of the fact that during the year '76 he held the anomalous position of revenue collector, collecting government taxes from people who were not recognized citizens and who resented the injustice, he still was one of the most popular men in camp.

Late in the winter following that Fourth of July petition, the prayer was granted and the Black Hills were officially opened to white men. Four years later all the saucy little camps running down Whitewood Gulch and sprawling up toward Gold Run were gathered together into the incorporated town of Deadwood. We called them by their original names for a long time—Cleveland, South Deadwood, Ingleside, Elizabethtown, Chinatown, Fountain City, and Montana City. Deadwood itself never had been planned nor named. Early prospectors called the gulch in which they found their richest placer diggings, Deadwood Gulch because of the burned timber on the mountain side above. They still talked about going "up to Deadwood Gulch," when the name included a cluster of cabins. As the camp became important enough to have a name, they gradually dropped the word "gulch" and the camp was thereafter Deadwood.

Forest Hill, sloping steeply up from the gulch on

A Little Girl in Old Deadwood

the west, was the only residence district included in the original Deadwood. The pines had been cut only where it was necessary for the building of the homes above their terraced dooryards on the three one-sided streets and at night the lamplights twinkled among the trees like friendly little stars. Williams street had been terraced out of the mountain and was the first as you went uphill. With no beginning and no end, it still was Forest Hill's one straight horizontal roadway. It appeared suddenly up on the hill above the flour mill in front of Henrico Livingstone's cabin, but it didn't begin there. It had come along obscurely from somewhere else. Henrico lived alone in a shabby little cabin and protected with a Winchester a mining claim she worked herself just back of the cabin. Sometimes she got into trouble with her gun. She had an unpleasant habit of throwing stones at the school children who strayed out of the school yard that backed up from Main street. I suppose she thought we wanted to jump her claim. The boys entered gayly into the stone throwing with the result that Miss Livingstone occasionally stalked, a tall grim figure, shabby, stiff, and dour, into the school room to lay her grievances before the principal. He always promised her courtesy and consideration, and ordered us to stay away from her. No one seemed ever to take into account that it always was Henrico who started the trouble. When I once called my father's attention to this, he said that he never had heard of her coming into the school yard to throw stones, and we had no business on her property nor any occasion to walk along the street in front of it. The surest way to keep out of trouble, he said, was not to run into it.

After leaving Henrico's warlike domain, Williams street swept its skirts clean between the Catholic and Baptist churches and by the time it came to the back fence of the school, was entirely fit for association with children. It was an excellent natural toboggan slide down to the corral and the bridge over City Creek after which it came into a confusion of corners where a lot of streets got off, with some difficulty, on their various ways.

The double line of houses that followed the little thread of a stream up a gently ascending gulch, had a nice name of some sort that no one ever remembered. We called it "City Crick." On one side of the road the houses were reached by long flights of ascending stairs. On the other, short flights went down to the front doors. So far as I know City Crick went on forever. In all the long wanderings of my childhood, I never came to the end of it, nor passed the last house. Away up, somewhere, a man named Tilley had a cabin, a cross dog, a mild little boy, and a claim on the public highway. Sometimes he shot at people who tried to cross his property but nothing serious ever came of it.

Centennial avenue, starting at that same corner, was a long diagonal trail that twisted and curved up past the residences on its high side until it came, after all sorts of queer detours, to the shoulder of the mountain where there was an isolated house and garden. On the way up it passed a little old log cabin where the door always was closed and padlocked. Some one told me that a prospector lived

A Little Girl in Old Deadwood

there, that he was away all day prospecting and that he had thousands of dollars in gold dust hidden behind the locked door. I never was able to verify this, and I doubted it, even then. We used to stop on our way to and from long climbs in the woods to rest on his doorstep and gather sheep sorrel. Mother said she could make a salad of it if we got enough, but in spite of our valiant efforts we never did. It grew only in that one place. I tried hard because I had a lively curiosity as to what a sheep-sorrel salad would be like. The only salads we knew anything about were of leaf lettuce, cabbage, and very rarely cucumbers, that we bought from a Chinaman who had a truck garden away down the gulch somewhere and peddled them around town in a little cart drawn by one horse. We made up for the sorrel deficiency by bringing in quantities of choke cherries, little gray-blue Oregon grapes that grew close to the ground, sarvis berries, and small red raspberries for pies. Living two hundred miles from a railroad in a country where no one troubled to raise fruit, we were dependent on the little wild berries we could gather, and the buffalo berries and wild plums the ranchers brought in from the valleys in the fall. My mother considered the lack of apples and peaches and grapes a serious deprivation. It grieved her, too, that our knowledge of woods was so limited in comparison with her own.

"My poor children," she used to say. "They know only two kinds of trees—pines and the others, whatever they may be."

She did us some injustice in that for we did know spruce from pines and we had a speaking acquaintance with birch and quaking aspens. But that she should feel sorry for us! That was the amazing thing. She whose childhood had been spent on an Ohio farm! She who had grown up in an *old* country that could not possibly have had any sympathy with children! We felt an unvoiced pity for her. Never as a child had she been friends with pines or climbed steep mountain sides thick with kinnikinick to come up on a divide and look down on all the world—on tumbled masses of mountains and sometimes even on clouds. She was of those who, as Badger Clark says, "never can understand the way we have loved you, young, young land."

She would have preferred to live where she had a large elm-shaded yard for her children to play in and long stretches of tree-shaded streets and country roads along which she could drive with her horse and buggy, her children piled in around her. Deadwood's drives were so narrow there always was difficulty when two drivers met, and they extended, for general daily driving, from tollgate to tollgate. When that grew monotonous one got reckless and paid two tolls and drove "around the belt," the triangle drive up Deadwood Gulch through Poorman Gulch to Lead, and back down Gold Run to Deadwood. If you went anywhere else, it was a long day's journey.

Shine street started from that confused corner and went down town on a slant past the Methodist Church and the old Wentworth Hotel and became something of a street in its own right. Its name was supposed to have been given it by some one who came from the capital of Wyoming but didn't know

A Little Girl in Old Deadwood

how to spell it and was a little forgetful of the number of syllables.

Williams street managed a couple of blocks more in the conventional fashion of having houses on both sides. It passed Lee street, a wide three-flighted stairway that dropped into an alley at the bottom of the hill and then picked itself up and went along like a regular street, cornering all the banks and being very important until it bumped into the foot of Mount Moriah just where Sherman street began.

Guy street catapulted down from Centennial with houses and stairs on either side of a rough perpendicular incline that was used for tobogganing in the winter and for nothing at all in the summer except on rare occasions when some reckless driver persuaded a strong, amiable team up or down.

At this point Williams street dropped her houses from the gulch side. They would have tumbled in anyway. A sidewalk with a railing ran along the edge of the hill, and twice stairways came up inquiringly from the gulch. After a comparatively long level stretch, the street lifted itself abruptly to "Nigger Hill" where one of the two colored families in town lived. Mrs. Goodrich was a kindly, mammy-like soul, and her children went to school and slid down hill with us. There was "Sad" Goodrich who got his nickname from his mother who, because he was not a merry infant, called him "ma sad baby," and the name clung to him always. There was Laura who was about my age and a little dark tower of strength. I remember one night when we were all coasting down Nigger Hill in the dark and I went over the side and halfway down to the bottom. I landed in a snowdrift and couldn't disentangle myself and I couldn't get any helpful attention from anybody until I heard Laura's soft, velvety voice. "Miss Estelline?" she called and when I shouted at the top of my lungs she came and pulled me and my sled out and took us back to the beaten track with apparently no effort at all.

"Old man Goodrich" wasn't as desirable a neighbor as the rest of the family. Once he brought a scurrying shooting scrap up into the narrow passageway between us and the house next door. I never did know what it was all about but there was a good deal of shooting and screaming and my little sister, Halle, and I followed the General when he ran out to see what it was all about. He saw her and told her to go back, but she didn't, and he never saw me, so we went on and peered down into the dark area way, the other house being considerably lower than our terraces. Pretty soon the General came back and the Goodriches went home and that was all there was to that. Nobody was killed and nobody was arrested. It was just one of Deadwood's ordinary little shooting scraps, that was all. The only unusual thing about it was that it didn't belong in our front yard.

If the children of lower Forest Hill came through their winters with whole heads and limbs, it was because the snow on the side hill was soft and deep and we grew so accustomed to tumbling about with our sleds that we didn't mind it. It required the utmost skill to keep in the street because it was so narrow. Teams could not pass and to make traffic of a sort possible a house every now and then stepped back accommodatingly and left space for a "turn-around."

From the top of the Goodrich's hill, Williams street paused a moment and then meandered off downward to nowhere in particular. Out in that direction there was a beautiful flat gray rock shadowed by a clump of pine trees. It was one of the most charming places in the world to sit on a summer day and meditate. The sounds of the town came up muted and mellow. Very faintly from Lead, three miles away, came the muffled roar of the Homestake stamp mills. The view of the town was beautiful, from the Hildebrand garden directly below, with its gorgeous masses of hollyhocks, to the mountains that shut in the gulch on every horizon. Hildebrand was a French Canadian with an express wagon and a large family of nice little boys who played with my brothers, and nowhere in all Deadwood Gulch was there such a flower garden as his, secluded behind his drab stone house and visible only from the hill above.

Forest Hill's second residence terrace was Forest avenue. It was no avenue at all, not even a street. It was just a sidewalk with houses fronting on it. They were very smart houses and the dwellers in them were very smart people. During the hectic mining stock boom of '86, it was known as "Iron Hill Row," because everybody who lived up there owned stock in Iron Hill, the silver mine out at Carbonate Camp that was so rich it started a new boom and kept it going. It paid dividends and did everything a mine should but it was a bad influence on the rest of Carbonate. It made every unscratched

19

little location think it was a mine too. It was responsible for a gay summer in Deadwood, however. There had not been so much money in circulation since the summer of '76. People gave large parties in their houses. McClintock built an Opera House over his livery barn with four boxes on each side of the stage and a repertoire company played to good business all summer.

Father said that brilliant bedazzling boom, the like of which had not been known since the original discovery of gold in Deadwood Gulch, was an illustration of the western passion for balance, justice, and contrast, because it followed the continuous blizzard that encircled the Hills the winter before when all the cattle on the open ranges died and all the cattlemen went broke.

Ingleside, which shared with Forest Hill the distinction of being the best resident district of Deadwood, was the less western of the two. It cuddled in the hollow of the mountains on the east side of the gulch and was farther away from the heart of the town by the bias length of Sherman street. Its houses were surrounded by little yards and gardens and its people could not look down each other's chimneys as we did on Forest Hill. Neither did they have our flashing glimpses of the mysterious life of the badlands. Mother thought that was an advantage to them but one that was offset somewhat by their daily walk up and down Sherman street, shabby, shiftless, and no better than it should be.

It was not until the streets of Deadwood were later outlined brilliantly with electric lights that I noticed how they lay in a perfect Y. It couldn't

MAIN STREET DEADWOOD 1876

Deadwood's main thoroughfare, showing a placer mine which occupied the middle of the roadway in 1876, to the left of the tailor shop.

(From a contemporary photograph.)

Earliest Picture of Deadwood Gulch

Showing the burnt-out timber on the hillside, which gave the place its name.

(From a print made when gold was discovered there in 1875.)

be seen in the first yellow lights, shining out casually here and there from saloons and stores and the windows of the houses. Main street running straight up the gulch was the stem. McGovern Hill, obtruding its huge dark bulk between Deadwood and Whitewood Gulches, cut the forks. Main street swerved and took its line of lights up Deadwood Creek, and Sherman street trundled along up Whitewood.

At the foot of McGovern Hill, crowded sideways against it, stood the Congregational Church, Deadwood's pioneer place of worship. It was a crude, simple building with uncertain turning stairs leading up to the door, and no effort at decoration, inside or out, but it had opened its doors in the summer of '77 and ever since its half-dozen unslumbering eyes had watched the gulch that stretched straight before it to the badlands, and its little basement assembly room had been an important social gathering place.

We lived on Williams street at the head of the Wall street stairs, in a story and a half frame house with a mansard roof, a square bay window, and a scrap of a porch reached by steps that started for the bay window and then changed their mind and turned and led to the front door. From our steps my little sister and brothers and I, the safe haven of our home behind us, could look down through the narrow slit to Main street and beyond to the foot of the mountain that stepped into Red Creek. Wall street was a naughty little thoroughfare that divided the good and the bad in Deadwood. It was known as the "dead-line" below which the police

Old Deadwood Days

never interfered after six o'clock at night, and at each end it ran into a house of the sort that did not exist above the dead-line. One of them, "the 400" huddled under the hill directly below us, its roof in plain view. When we climbed down the steep hillside after chokecherries or a lost ball, we could see the darkly curtained windows but we never could get a glimpse inside. The house at the other end perched perilously over the creek and when the big flood came, it went down with the current. This might have served to point a moral if it had not been that the schoolhouse and the Methodist Church went too, while the Gem Theater and a lot of saloons stood fast.

Once I was sent on some imperative errand in the early evening guarded by our big dog, Danger. I was perfectly safe for two reasons. Danger didn't allow anyone to walk on the same side of the street with me as far as he could see them, and all good women and little girls were a sacred trust to Deadwood. But coming back I came through Wall street and up the long flight of stairs that ended at our doorstep and in its steep ascent ran the whole gamut of human morals. Back of one of the proud buildings on the corner that turned a haughty shoulder to Wall street and pretended it belonged only to Main street, was a row of three little one-story, dingy, white houses. They were so small that each front had room for only a door and one window. The night that I came that way with Danger, one of the doors stood open. A kerosene lamp shone gayly through a red shade, and in its circle of light a girl lay, apparently asleep, on a couch. She had a pretty, delicate young face with long dark lashes lying against her cheek. Masses of wavy dark hair fell over her elaborate, lace-trimmed pink *negligée*. I stopped to look at her until Danger growled and I hurried on up the stairs. She was a picture I never forgot and for years did not understand, but for some reason that I could not have explained, I never spoke of her to anyone, not even to Irene, my chum, with whom I held long and frequent naïve discussions concerning the badlands and their careless, mysterious inhabitants.

Home looked very cozy and dear and safe when I came in out of the dark. Mother was sitting in front of the fireplace with Mrs. Mather—pretty, gray-haired, gentle Mrs. Mather—and they were talking about the church supper next week. Mrs. Mather said Mrs. Hastie would make an angel cake and she was the "boss angel of this town." Mother was mending a pair of small trousers. She said she would make some lemon jelly and that Irene and I would wear French peasant costumes and wait on the table.

From the dining room came the light clink of silver and china. Our Norwegian maid, Alamena Marie, was setting the table. Mother told me to go out and tell her to put on an extra plate. Mrs. Mather was staying for dinner because Mr. Mather was out at the mine and wouldn't be home until late. I came back and sat down on a pile of floor pillows beside my mother. She paid no attention to me but that didn't matter. Her soft voice went on exchanging kindly gossip with Mrs. Mather and I wondered if the sleeping girl I had seen through the open door could have had a mother anything like her.

We saw a good deal of interest go by the little rift of Wall street. We used to watch the stagecoach come in with a proud flourish, and the long trains of patient bull teams with their covered freight wagons pull slowly up the street. We counted the wagons and oxen as they passed and made small wagers with each other as to their number. We were natural born gamblers all of us. We played poker for matches and whoever lost had to go to bed in the dark. We did that until Father stopped us because he said he didn't want the boys to learn to gamble. He didn't think Halle and I would carry it to the danger point. One summer later on, when Mother and the other three children were down at the Springs, I acquired the habit of going with Irene and Mose Lyon and Louis Caulfield out to the races every day. I bet on St. Patrick's Day because of his name and his beauty and I won a lot of money. I think it was four dollars. It was so much that I couldn't conceal the possession of it from my father and he put a stop to that too. But counting oxen and covered wagons was a slow, quiet amusement. The stagecoach arrival was different. That was the grand excitement of the day as long as we were a stagecoach town. Its six white horses came up the gulch on a gallop. The driver on his high seat flourished his long whip in skillful skyward sweeps, the dingy white canvas-covered coach lurched and rolled from side to side with its distinctive rumble and our one brief daily tangency with the far world beyond the mountains and across the plains swaggered to an

A Little Girl in Old Deadwood

abrupt stop in front of the Merchants Hotel. The stagecoach was the herald from the world that lay beyond the White Rocks and the tumbled mountains that rolled up around them. It brought a four-day-old Chicago paper, letters from strange places beyond the Missouri River, and passengers who as recently as last week had seen a locomotive and a train of cars. Sometimes it brought capitalists with money to develop mines. We could hear it coming while it still was a long way down the gulch and always we rushed to the window or the front steps, according to the weather, to watch its disjointed dash past Wall street—four horses at a time and then the other two and the coach. That's how narrow Wall street was. It was a wonderful experience to be on the wooden-canopied porch of the Merchants Hotel when the stagecoach arrived. I wanted to go down there every day and wait for it, but that wasn't my mother's idea of proper conduct for a little girl.

I was sure that Father and the General never told us everything that happened. For instance, there was the woman with her three children who came in to meet her husband only to find that he had shot himself that afternoon. I didn't know the man and I don't remember his name, but the General said he had lent him money two or three times during the winter because he said he was expecting his family that day on the coach. Father said he had given him money on several occasions for the same reason. He had borrowed it that way from nearly every man in town and never did the family come, until that day when nobody believed him and he could borrow

25

Old Deadwood Days

no more. He was a gambler with poor luck and the day the family finally came he didn't have even the price of a meal. Father and the General couldn't make up their minds whether they were glad or sorry that he hadn't asked them that last day. They were afraid they might have refused like the others and been filled with regret. On the other hand, they might have given it to him and there would have been no tragedy. Mother thought it was too bad he hadn't seen one of them.

Then there was the time an old prospector from somewhere up around Ragged Top came down to meet a woman with whom he had corresponded through a matrimonial paper, and when he saw her, she was so homely he ran away. She identified him by his running and went after him, and he had to marry her anyway. I never heard how it turned out.

If the stage was on time, Deadwood's dinners were on the table by the time the mail was distributed and the men got home. If it were late, the whole schedule of our daily life was disordered. And sometimes it was several days late! It had a thousand good reasons for delays even though Indians had ceased troubling when the treaty was signed, and road agents, the masked highwaymen of the Hills, had abandoned their nefarious practices. More than nine hundred and ninety-nine of these reasons had to do with the heavy gumbo roads through the real Badlands—not Deadwood's moral badlands. Sometimes the Cheyenne River swelled and rose so that the ford was impassable for days. It was not an easy journey from Sidney

A Little Girl in Old Deadwood

or from Pierre. No wonder the horses, the stage, and the driver were proud and boastful when finally they reached Deadwood.

Below the badlands, Chinatown twisted along its narrow picturesque way, housing the largest Chinese population ever achieved by any town of the size of Deadwood, outside of China. In the shabby little shops were piled great quantities of beautiful Oriental silks, embroideries, egg-shell china, sandalwood, teak and carved ivory. There were innumerable laundry shops. The clothes of Deadwood were as thoroughly washed as the gravel in the creek. There were gambling games that no one interfered with—naturally, considering the number that ran wide open for the pleasure, profit, and occasional tragedy of the white man. A joss house painted brown with little red embellishments pointed and peaked and squared itself in unexpected ways and places. On the outside it was unlike anything else in all the Black Hills. The inside we were never permitted to see. A peculiar and intriguing odor of incense came to meet you a block away. Its religious hold on the Chinese was not universal, however, for many of them came to the Chinese school at the Congregational Church and one, expressing his new faith through his art, ornamented a wedding cake with raised pink sugar letters explaining that "God made the world but Wong made this cake."

My father was the unofficial counsel for the Chinese and the connection was valuable to us in many ways. Always in emergencies he could commandeer a cook or dishwasher on a moment's notice.

Old Deadwood Days

When there was not a Chinese servant to be had in the whole gulch, one would spring up from some dark corner at Father's bidding and come cheerfully into our kitchen. They were real Chinese in those days too, wearing queues wound round their heads and loose, dull-blue trousers, and long shirts. At Christmas time and on both their New Year's Day and our own, dozens of Chinamen brought us rare and lovely gifts of an infinite variety from embroidered crêpe shawls and Satsuma teapots, to scarlet chopsticks which we tried hard to use but were discouraged by the family, especially Mother, because of the amount of rice we spilled over the tablecloth.

Father's service to his Chinese clients consisted entirely in seeing that they were given fair trials when they were arrested for selling opium. I think he always managed an acquittal. Neither judicial nor public opinion was very strong about such things. If a Chinamen wanted to smoke opium, who cared? They rarely were in trouble about anything else. I remember once, in my later teens, I slipped into a night police court with Father because, as we were coming home from prayer meeting, a Chinese client stopped him, and he didn't know what else to do with me. A Chinaman had quarreled with a gambler by the name of "Little Gus," over a white woman, and Little Gus had emerged from the affair so much the worse for the Chinaman's bread knife, that his friends demanded speedy justice against the "chink." I never forgot Little Gus's face as he sat in that basement court room dimly lighted with a few inadequate kerosene lamps. The white bandage around his head intensi-

A Little Girl in Old Deadwood

fied his pallor and his beautiful dark-lashed blue eyes as he lifted them to Judge Early on the bench were innocent as a baby's. He had the face of an angel but a record in the badlands that acquitted the Chinaman.

When Wing Tsue, the leading Chinese merchant, brought his wife from China, he announced to the white men of his acquaintance that she would be at home on their New Year's Day and he would be glad if the wives of his friends would call on her. They did. I went with my mother. We were ushered in through Wing Tsue's dim, fragrant store and up a steep outside stairway to the small ordinary looking house that clung to the hill and gave no evidence of the warm luxury within. The apartment in which our hostess received us was heavily curtained and draped, richly furnished in teak and enamel, and the air was thick with the odor of sandalwood and Chinese punk. Mrs. Wing Tsue herself was the loveliest bit of exquisite china I ever saw. She was painted and mascaraed in a way no nice American woman could understand in those days but on her the effect was charming. Her black hair was built in a high pyramid with gorgeous pins and combs. Her brilliant silk jacket and trousers were heavy with embroidery, and her tiny useless little feet were encased in embroidered satin shoes with wooden soles. She spoke no English but her gentle gracious manners and her courteous solicitude about the serving of tea and the delectable little almond cakes, small candied limes, and other bonbons made us feel as if we had talked over all the polite topics of the day with her.

Old Deadwood Days

She returned our calls a few weeks later, driving out in the finest carriage behind the highest-stepping team that could be commandeered from Job Lawrenson's livery barn, and Job Lawrenson, a pioneer, had the best horses and equipages in the Black Hills. I am sure it was the only time she ever left her rich, close rooms. But her children went to the public school and to Sunday school. She was the only "respectable" Chinese woman that ever came to Deadwood. Later she and her little girls went back to China and after a while Wing Tsue and the boy joined them. But that was a long while after.

The other Chinese women—the ones that Mrs. Wing Tsue did not know—lived in the "cribs" along that part of Main street that ran through Chinatown, and beckoned to passers-by. But they could not have belonged to the underworld for the term was not used in Deadwood. Everything was too open and aboveboard.

The gayest thing about the Chinese was their funerals. They marched up Main street and Sherman, and around up the steep Ingleside way that led to the cemetery on Mount Moriah, scattering little red pieces of paper with Chinese characters on them. They were intended to distract the attention of the devil away from the dead, some one told us, and we gathered them up with much interest. Always marching with the Chinese in their funeral processions was Dr. von Wedelstaedt, the one white man who belonged to the Chinese masons. He was a tall, straight, dignified Prussian, family physician to half of Deadwood, and carrying a personal interest not only in our health, for which he felt entirely responsible, but in our general welfare no less.

"Don't look so cross all the time," he used to tell me. "Be pleasant like your sister." And to Halle, "Why don't you stand up straight like your sister? You'll have to stand up straight or you can't marry my boy, Bismarck."

He had jet black hair and whiskers and when he marched with the Chinese he wore his high silk hat, swung his goldheaded cane, and threw his head and shoulders back, proud of being the only man of his race among the Chinese masons. But he never could learn to eat with chopsticks. When he went to eat bird's nest soup and dried ducks with his friends he carried a spoon in his pocket.

At the other end of Main street, the Indians who used to come from the Pine Ridge and Rosebud reservations to attend United States court pitched their tepees and received their guests. We were a very friendly people in Deadwood. We went to see everybody who came to town. On one of these visits a hospitable group of squaws insisted that I join their dance and we shuffled and hopped around the fire to the wailing music one of them made on a queer little instrument, and we were just as chummy and happy as though we spoke the same language and our forefathers had not believed that the West was too small for two races. We had come so far in the late nineteenth century as to believe that Deadwood Gulch was wide enough for as many races as could find it. My squaw friends couldn't speak any more English than Mrs. Wing Tsue could, but between the little Oriental in her dim, stuffy, scented rooms, and the Indian squaws in their wind-swept, fire-lit tepees with the stars shining in, there was a distance greater than the length of all the Main streets in America linked together. Between them came all the rest of us—miners, lawyers, stage drivers, merchants, gamblers, doctors, priests, saloon keepers; women with their memories of older, gentler lands, and children growing up with their minds and hearts full of the glory of the old mountains and the charm of the young camp; men from the farms and villages of the prairie states, and men from the "effete east," political exiles from Europe and remittance men from England, and men whose pasts could not travel by stage. We were all children of the present and the future. No one was ever curious in old Deadwood. No one ever asked a man "what his name was back in the states."

A Deadwood Judge

Chapter 2

A DEADWOOD JUDGE

EADWOOD was growing out of its placer gold youth in the spring of 1877. It was beginning to ship gold bullion which is more dignified and sophisticated than gold dust. The Sioux, having ratified the treaty ceding the Black Hills to the palefaces, had gone sullenly, perhaps, but quietly back to their reservations and hung up their war bonnets and tomahawks. Not until their sons grew up, went to college, and studied treaty law, did they again question the ownership of the Hills. Then they did it around a council fire with a peace pipe passed to the Congressman who was their guest.

Silently and stealthily along the old war trail where the Indians had whooped and yelled, crept the road agents behind their black masks. The stageways into Deadwood were still as dangerous as they ever had been, but the town itself was a little less quick on the trigger. It was settling a new set of sins on the other shoulder. Crimes were classified curiously. Most murders were justified.

The man who killed Wild Bill had been brought to justice and hanged in Yankton but that was because he'd shot him in the back. Usually the victim was buried and there was an end of it. Road agents were sent to the penitentiary if they were caught. If a man stole a horse he was hanged immediately by whomever happened to be around. If by any chance it sometimes proved to be the wrong man, that was his misfortune. He should have been more careful about the company he kept. Horse stealing was the worst sort of murder because it left a man at the mercy of every enemy, from an Indian down to hunger and cold. An unhorsed man in the West was as helpless as a lame duck in a desert. There were no petty crimes. Pickpockets, burglars, embezzlers, and night-slinking thieves never possess the daring required to operate two hundred slow miles from a railroad.

The one baffling crime of that restless, perplexed year of '77 concerned the ownership of mining claims. A miner's staked-out bit of hope was his only as long as his neighbor was honest. There were no mining laws and claim-jumping was coming to be a popular pastime. A prospector held his ground by sitting on it or by digging day and night. His location notice was nothing more than a stick and a scrap of paper.

The placer mines that yielded the gold of '76 were above ground in the sunlight. It was not easy to trifle with them. But when men began running tunnels and sinking shafts and doing their mining by dim candle-light under ground, it seemed to be more difficult to distinguish their own gold from their neighbors'. Sometimes even honest men forgot or mislaid their boundaries.

Into this mêleé of mining entanglements came my father, Granville G. Bennett, in the spring of 1877,

A Deadwood Judge

and in August he held the first term of Federal Court in a log cabin at Sheridan.

He never talked much about that pioneer term of court but a framed picture of the cabin hung over his office desk as long as he lived. After the one term at Sheridan the court was moved to Deadwood.

Sheridan was a log-cabin scrap of a town in the lovely valley of Spring Creek, one of the richest placer streams in the Hills. From one claim there in the fall of '75 three thousand dollars was washed in one week including a nugget worth $23.00. The guns had just been taken out of the cabin portholes where they had been trained on warring Indians during '75 and '76 and the town was all aglow with golden hopes of wealth and greatness when Father drove in with the United States marshal and the clerk of the court. Room and board had been arranged for him in one of the cabins by the lawyers who rode in on horseback over hard mountain trails, slept where they could and ate in what was called a restaurant.

It is significant that the Sioux, having signed the treaty by which they lost the land they believed to be the hunting ground of the Great Spirit, rode away philosophically to their tepee fires on the flat prairie reservations without a backward glance at the glorious purple mountains, while the palefaces immediately started such a wrangle trying to snatch each other's little shares in the golden ground that the Great White Father's courts were kept busy trying to maintain peace among his own white children.

On the first day of that first term of court in

Old Deadwood Days

Sheridan a man was convicted of robbery and turned over to the United States marshal for safe keeping until the court should pronounce sentence. The prisoner, the marshal, witnesses, jurors, and lawyers slept in a log cabin that had no floor. The marshal and his prisoner lay down together and went to sleep. They were tired and the crisp, high-altitude autumn air was conducive to sound sleep. When the marshal woke in the morning, the prisoner was gone. He had crawled out through a hole that had been dug under the bottom log of the cabin wall. No one ever heard of him again. Either he learned from that one experience to let other people's property alone, or he grew wise in the ways of not being caught.

In October, the United States court was transferred to Deadwood and Father held court in the Bonanza building on Sherman street, using for a bench a homemade wooden chair in which were roughly cut the words: "Made for Judge Bennett, first term of court in Deadwood, October, 1877." Its workmanship offended the artistic sense of Judge McLaughlin and of Noah Seiver who was bailiff and in less than a month Father came into court one morning to find a fine easy armchair that gave Sheriff Seth Bullock occasion to express the opinion that "the presentation was wrong; that the *particeps criminis* having tried undue influence upon the head of his honor and failed, now applied their efforts to the very seat of justice."

The Black Hills was my father's kind of country. He was a pioneer and builder to the very heart of him. Each generation of his family had come a

A Deadwood Judge

little farther west, since the first pioneers fared forth
from Ireland and one straggled down from Scotland
to join them and marry into the family. He himself
made four westward moves—from Ohio where he
was born, to Illinois and Iowa with his parents while
he still was a boy, to Vermillion, Dakota Territory
when he was appointed one of the three Federal
Judges of the territory, and, later, to the Black Hills.
Probably he would have made a fifth if Deadwood
had not remained, up until his old age, a frontier
town. Perhaps, too, he found something there that
had held his grandfather's heart in Ireland and
never had been recaptured in the tame level lands of
the middle states. He came with the love of new
land in his heart and the authority of the United
States Government in his hands. The West that was
dear to him was not the gun-playing, law-defying
frontier, but the young, pliant, enthusiastic country
from which a great state could be built.

Qualities inherited from his pioneering Irish and
Scotch ancestors made my father one of the notable
judges of the West. From the Irish he brought a
fire, a stirring love of adventure without which no
one could have endured the hardships of the early
Hills life, and a vivid colorful imagination that I
am sure peopled the forests and gulches with fairies
and gave him a far vision that crept into his "Codes
of '77," and his interpretation of mining laws that
had to be created as the need arose. He never took
quite the same interest in the law after it became a
fixed and settled thing safely ensconced between calf
bindings.

It was the Irish in him that coated his tongue with

39

silver and made him one of the resplendent lights of the Deadwood bar—a bar famous throughout the West during the late 'seventies and 'eighties for its brilliant oratory and its wide knowledge of the fine points of mining law.

Considering the prominent place mining litigation had on the court dockets and in the life of the community, it was surprising to find an occasional miner who knew nothing about it. An old prospector named Pat was trying once to sell his claims in Two Bit Gulch to Father for one of his capitalist clients. Father listened a little abstractedly until Pat finished his story of a widening vein of high-grade ore and the certainty of another Homestake over there behind White Rocks, if only Father's client would invest a few dollars and develop the proposition—just a few dollars, not more than half a million or so. Prospectors always think in figures like that.

When he was all through Father answered him casually: "I can't touch your ground, Pat. It's in litigation."

"It's a domned lie," Pat retorted indignantly; "it's in porphyry."

It was the same Pat who stopped Father on the street one day just after we had had a fresh coat of paint on our house. "Sure, Judge, and I always thought you was Irish," he said. "It's a good old Irish name you've got. I know a whole den of Bennetts back in the old country. And you look Irish. You've got the black-ringed blue eyes and the black hair. I always thought you was Irish, but now I know it. I just walked up along Williams street,

A Deadwood Judge

and I saw your house. There never was anything so green outside of Ireland unless it belonged to an Irishman."

Father had been thinking of toning down the shade a little, but after that he glowed with pride of race every time he looked at the house.

From the Scotch strain he brought to the bench a sense of righteous rectitude that influenced into straight uncompromising lines all his decisions, both judicial and personal. One of these concerned the kindly offer of a block of stock in a rich new mining company whose mine already was an established gold producer.

A friend of Father's who was an owner in the mine came to him one day in '77 when he was on the Federal bench and said: "Judge, you ought to have some of this Homestake stock. You don't get a salary that will make you rich and you have children who will be getting more expensive every year. The stock is low now but it's going to be worth a lot of money before very long, and it's going to be paying big dividends for a great many years." Even he could not have realized then how many. "Take a couple of thousand shares and hang onto them and you'll find them very handy some day."

"No," Father said, "you are right when you say my salary won't make me rich. It won't even permit me to speculate—or," when his friend would have interrupted him, "make investments. I couldn't afford to buy two shares, let alone two thousand."

The friend said that had nothing to do with it. The company would be glad to carry his two thousand shares for him as long as it might be necessary.

Father could not do that. It would have been a light nebulous entanglement that might have hampered his just decision if the Homestake mining company ever had brought a lawsuit into his court. As it happened, it never did. Yet in spite of the fact that he lived to see the stock multiply its value incredibly, and watched it pay dividends all his life, he never, even in his most financially disturbed moments, regretted that decision. He never thought anything at all about it unless some one recalled it to him.

"It would be nice if we had that Homestake stock that you scorned," I suggested to him once when we were trying to figure ways and means on our low family exchequer.

"Not at that price," he replied firmly.

"But they never did have a case before you."

"I couldn't know that."

"But if they had, couldn't you have called in another judge or something?"

"That would have been a dishonorable evasion. It wouldn't have been playing fair with them."

Probably it was the blend of Scotch and Irish that was responsible for two outstanding beliefs that were as fixed in my father's mind as the north star over our roof tree. He was opposed absolutely to capital punishment with a conviction based on a belief in the fifth commandment. That did not say, he contended, that you should not kill except by due process of law. It made no exceptions or explanations at all. It merely charged: "Thou shalt not kill." Furthermore, it was not one of the old Testament laws that had been abrogated in the new. During his years on the bench he never had sentenced a man to be hanged and if it had come to an issue, he would have resigned rather than have sent any man to the gallows.

"Whether or not a man deserves death," he said, "is a question for God alone to decide."

He could condemn a man to hard labor for life with no compunction whatever. That, he thought, came within the province of the court.

Another steadfast conviction that brought down upon his fine shapely head the wrath of earnest reformers was that a child belonged with its mother no matter who she was, where she lived, or how she behaved.

"I believe," he said once, in rendering a decision in which he gave a baby into the custody of its disreputable mother, "that the Lord knows where He sends children and it is not the intention of this court to take issue with the decrees of the Almighty."

His unfaltering faith in a personal God was illustrated vividly to me when I was a very little girl. My sister, Halle, just younger than I, had been very ill through several weeks of a summer unusually hot for the Hills. The doctor came several times a day and the household was tense and gloomy. On this particular late afternoon Mother had come downstairs with the doctor and she and Father talked to him for a few minutes in the hall before he left. She was crying, I noticed, when she went upstairs. I stood on the top step of the front porch when the doctor went out. He did not even see me. He went quickly down the steps, his head and shoulders up and swinging his cane, but I noticed he flicked his eyes with his big silk handkerchief. In all the long years of his practice, old Dr. von Wedelstaedt never got used to grief.

I was standing there lonely and puzzled and unhappy when Father came out and took my hand. "Come take a little walk with me," he said; "I want to talk to you."

We walked up the street to the top of the hill where there were no houses, only pine trees, and looked down on Deadwood Gulch going about its concerns just as though there were no threatening shadow across our door.

"The doctor says Halle can't get well," he said in a quiet voice that choked a little. "He thinks she may not live through the night."

Only twice before had Death stalked into my short little life; once vaguely and impersonally when my mother had told me that Mabel French, a child I knew, was dead. I was a little awed and I always remembered because it was my first personal acquaintance with death. When I was about three, my grandfather died and I was filled with amazement because my mother and grandmother and my aunt cried. I thought something wonderful had happened to him, and they ought to be rejoicing. But Halle! Now I understood. I noticed a little row of stones not far away, where we had started to build a playhouse on the hill just before she was taken sick. Close beside it one little wild rose was blooming. I had seen that belated bud a few days before and planned to come up and get it for her as soon as it bloomed. And now she never would build playhouses nor pick roses. Everything in the world was tied up with her. Life couldn't go on without her. All this went through my mind in the instant my father paused. He went on with a lift in his voice that had not been there before. "But I think," he said, "that God hears the prayers of little children and answers them. If you ask Him to make Halle well, I'm sure He will."

I said my prayers at my grandmother's knee that night as I had for several nights, feeling a little neglected by my mother, but to-night it was all right. I understood.

"And now here's something," I told her at the end of the Amen, "that I want to say to God just alone," and she nodded. She was crying too. "Don't cry, Grandma," I reassured her almost gayly, "it's going to be all right."

Once in the night I heard the doctor come in and I got out of bed and said my prayer over again. In the morning Halle was better, incredibly, miraculously better. The doctor wiped his eyes and told Father it only went to show that doctors never knew as much as they thought they did. They had no business to make such definite statements. The medicine last night had worked better than he thought it could. Father and I looked at each other. We knew.

I watched my little sister grow well and strong as a matter of course. My father's faith had left no shadow of a doubt in my heart.

He was one of the pillars of the pioneer church that was opened in the summer of '77, a bare, grim little church at the foot of McGovern Hill where it could keep its half-dozen unslumbering eyes on the gulch stretching straight downstream before it and growing wickeder as it proceeded. The first floor assembly room started in front with pleasant daylight but backed darkly into the hill. In the church, reached by a twisting outside stairway, there were windows on every side. In front they looked serenely down the gulch. Through the opposite windows we lifted our eyes against a steep mountain side. We could have reached through if it had been permitted, which it was not, and picked a wild rose or a bit of poverty weed. They grew almost on the window sills.

Father sat with grave dignity at the head of his pew and church attendance in the morning was compulsory in our family. His knowledge of the Bible was prodigious and he used quotations from it plentifully and with telling effect in the many speeches he made both in and out of court. It was his insistence upon our acquiring Bible knowledge and the quantity and quality of his private library that gave his children the best of their early education. It was a wonderful library housed in a bookcase of father's own designing, and built to his own measurements. He had learned the carpenter's trade in his youth and prided himself on the use to which he could put it. The bookcase was of walnut in simple classic lines and filled one entire wall of our back parlor. Neither Father nor Mother dreamed, when they first filled it with books, that it would not always be adequate for all the books they would own. But the library had overflowed out of it into other bookcases and shelves until it seemed there

A Deadwood Judge

was not another corner in the house where a book might be tucked away. And still Father continued to buy them.

There was no public library in Deadwood in those days and there was no private library that compared with Father's. Mother had a good many books of her own and as we came along we added our little volumes, but the library always expressed Father. It was filled with histories, biographies, essays, and poetry. I remember long rows of Carlyle, Macaulay, Plato, and Froude, and a many volumed work on "The Rise and Fall of the Dutch Republic." His favorite poets, Burns, Shelley, Moore, and Byron, were bound in substantial calf like law books. He had Ecce Homo and Ecce Deus, the interesting though spurious Ossian, and everything written by Thoreau and Ik Marvel. There was nothing of Renan, Tom Payne, Voltaire, or Ingersoll, and there was very little fiction. Father thought most fiction was frivolous and a waste of time. His high regard for women—their brains, and their right to suffrage or anything else they wanted, was shown in his library by such books as the complete works of Gail Hamilton.

He had a passion for owning books, and he not only owned them but he read and re-read them. Few men, I find, have the amount of accurate literary knowledge stored in their minds that he had. His own literary gift was not negligible but, with the exception of a few speeches that were printed and the editorials and special articles he wrote now and then for the local paper, his writing never achieved print. His attitude toward his work was

Old Deadwood Days

the same as it was toward his own personal popularity. People ought to like him and if they didn't, that was their loss. He would make no effort. It was the quality that interfered with his political life. Once, at the urgent solicitation of his family, he wrote an article on "Mining Laws" and sent it to a magazine. When it was returned, he threw it into the fireplace and never tried again. He "would not peddle his work." He wrote verses to all of us—exquisite bits of sentiment that his Scotch great-grandmother would not let him express in words.

In the evenings when the family was alone, he used to play the guitar and sing old songs—"Ben Bolt," "Kathleen Mavourneen," "I Dreamt I Dwelt in Marble Halls." He loved all simple tuneful music but he was certain that no one really liked grand opera. They couldn't. When I got old enough, I played his accompaniments on the piano. No one who has lived all his life within reach of professional music knows just how hard we worked to make our own music. Some obscure political entanglement in Germany sent us an unusually good piano teacher, and all the little girls in the camp learned not only to play, but to know something of operas and symphonies. This teacher used to give us *fantasias* from the operas and tell us the stories. He had seen "Aïda" when it was presented first in Cairo at the Imperial Opera House before the Khedive. People said he was a political exile. Halle and I owe our musical education to the fact that he was a client of Father's.

Father did not stop with the buying and reading of Gail Hamilton and a few other strong-minded

A Deadwood Judge

women. He espoused casually, but surely, the cause of woman's suffrage while it was yet an unpopular young weakling. Most western men believed in it. They were a sturdy race, doing the sort of things that brought them into no competition with women who were so scarce anyway that men thought they should have whatever they wanted and more too, for that matter. Most of them were not interested in voting. It was the chivalric attitude of the men that gave the vote to the few women there were in Wyoming in the early 'seventies. Father's convictions in the matter led him to bring home to dinner one night a suffrage speaker at whose meeting he had presided the night before. He had not been able to persuade Mother to go and hear her. None of us liked her very much. I don't think he did himself but she represented a principle he was trying to introduce into his household. He was horrified, and Mother and I were amused and a little justified in our opinion, when she went down to Hot Springs for a week-end a few days later with a lawyer of slack reputation.

Neither this incident, however, nor that of the crazy man who was his guest one night discouraged or deflected his broad, easy hospitality. We thought the man was crazy at the time but Father was very contemptuous of our aspersions. He said he had just opened up a vein of rattlesnakes and expected to get rich off them. Father gave him credit for trying to be witty. He said he had known him for a long time. He was a little queer, but perfectly sane. They sent him to the asylum the next week.

Mother said once that Father brought home to

dinner every man he met on the street. Dinner never was served in our family for just the number expected. Any of us could bring home anyone we liked at any time. It made for considerable gayety and sometimes, though rarely, a little merry confusion when we all brought in our friends at once without warning. That was one thing a maid in our house had to understand. A Chinaman did, as a matter of course. Father was the official attorney for Chinatown, and he could do no wrong in the eyes of the Chinese.

Our dinner table was never dull even when we were alone. Father and the General talked incessantly—about politics, mining, and the books they were reading. The General read novels which he kept secreted in his room. Breakfast was a haphazard meal that rarely assembled us all at one time. Luncheon was hurried. But at dinner we all were there. We had to be. And important and exciting things were discussed. Mother was inclined to be quiet and the rest of us were encouraged to follow her example. But we didn't do it. We went about during the day talking to all sorts of people, and we read books that we thought nobody else knew about in order to bring something to the dinner table that was of sufficient interest to command attention. We could talk as much as we liked if we had anything interesting to say. Otherwise, just as we got fairly started some one—Father, Mother, or the General, would stop us with the biting comment that, "Nobody wants to hear about that," and we would subside.

The General tossed the bomb about Matt Plunkett

A Deadwood Judge

fairly into the soup one night at dinner. It was news that couldn't wait.

"Matt Plunkett's going to run for Sheriff," he said.

"What!" Father almost choked on his first spoonful. "That old lawbreaker? It's a fine Sheriff he'll make when he can't obey the law himself."

The laws of the state of South Dakota which Father had helped to draft and all law that he was sworn by his profession to uphold were as sacred to him as the Ten Commandments. And he thought just as highly of the Commandments as Moses did. A lawbreaker was a scoundrel no matter what law he broke or how he did it. There were no small infringements. He thought it was all right once when a man was sent to the penitentiary for three years for stealing a pie. He had to pry open a window to get it, father said, and that was burglary. And anyway stealing a pie was a theft just as much as stealing a hoist off a mine. But even knowing all this I was sure from the way Father spoke that Matt Plunkett had stolen a bunch of horses, strangled a baby, gone down in the badlands and got drunk, and shot a nice man in the back.

The story as it unrolled between the two men at our table developed none of these crimes. He had tried to steal a mine—not the gold out of it, but the hole in the ground itself. Plunkett had been foreman of a mine in Hidden Treasure Gulch, they said, in the fall of '77 and some dispute about wages arose between the miners and the owners. Under the foreman's leadership, the disgruntled miners moved into the tunnel in which they had been working and

51

prepared to stay until things were settled to their satisfaction. They made preparations for a long sojourn. They took their beds, bedding, cooking utensils, and supplies from their cabins into the tunnel. They even moved their little cookstove and set it up near the air shaft which they used for a flue, and settled down for a comfortable stay. They were reckoning without judge and sheriff. The owners, apparently having right on their side, appealed to the court and father sent Sheriff Seth Bullock out armed with the authority of the law, to dispossess the tenants of the tunnel.

The rebels, safely entrenched, cared nothing at all about the law. The sheriff thundered threats down the air shaft at them but they didn't trouble to answer him. They stayed like bed rock. United States troops, reinforcing the sheriff and his deputies, failed to make any more impression than if they had been a gang of schoolboys with sling shots.

Father's righteous Irish wrath rose high. Who did these men think they were to defy the law in this way? Seth Bullock set his firm jaw and was silent. Neither boded well for the rebel miners.

"Bullock," Father said after things had gone on for several days, "you'll have to go and get those fellows out. There must be no bloodshed, but otherwise I don't care how you do it."

A nice thing to ask of an old Montana *vigilante,* that he quell disorder without pulling a gun or even throwing a stone that might hit a fellow's nose and make it bleed. Judge Bennett's aversion to bloodshed was well known. It was something about which he felt definitely just as he did about capital punish-

GUARDING HIS PLACER
CLAIM DEADWOOD GULCH
1876

The best placer claim in Deadwood Gulch was Number 2, below Discovery.
It was so rich it had to be guarded constantly by a man with a Winchester,
and in less than four months gave its owners nearly $150,000.

(*From a contemporary photograph.*)

A Deadwood Judge

ment. Sheriff Bullock had a resourceful mind. If he couldn't draw blood in this miserable quiet battle, he would do something else equally effective, and he would do it without any preliminary talk. He went up to the stronghold in Hidden Treasure Gulch, left his deputies at the mouth of the tunnel, and climbed the mountain side to the place where the smoke came out of the air shaft. Quietly, with a crafty little smile hiding under his long mustache, the sheriff dropped one by one his missiles of offense through the chimney into the fire. Fragments of an odor that might have originated in the infernal regions a little farther down, came up the air shaft, but the greater volume stayed inside and the miners, vanquished and disgusted, poured out of the mouth of the tunnel, just as Seth Bullock had known they would. They held their noses tight against this unexpected onslaught. Their heads were bowed but not in the least bloody. The sheriff had dropped asafetida into the rebel camp.

Father chuckled delightedly over that bloodless victory all the rest of his life. It verified and strengthened his high regard for Seth Bullock, who set a standard then to which all other sheriffs, so far as Father was concerned, had to measure. His friendly esteem was not limited to Mr. Bullock's law-enforcing ability. They went through a great deal together, and it was no idle compliment that a railroad official in later years paid them when he said: "It was the Bennetts and Bullocks that brought law and order into the Black Hills."

When the Spanish War came, Seth Bullock went as a captain of Rough Riders under his personal friend, Colonel Roosevelt. And once in Chicago, a long time after, I attended a small tea that Mrs. Roosevelt gave in her hotel sitting room when she was in the city with Mr. Roosevelt for a national convention. I happened to sit nearest the door so that when the Great American came in for a few moments, he sat down beside me and asked me where I came from. When I told him Deadwood, with all the high pride of a Bourbon or a Plantagenet, he asked if I knew his friend, Captain Seth Bullock.

"You know," he said, "that when I came back from my trip around the world, I sent for him to meet me in London." Certainly I had known all about that.

"Do you know why I sent for him? Because I wanted those Britishers to see my ideal typical American."

That was Seth Bullock, tall, lean, with drooping mustache, keen gray eyes, a whimsical humor, a soft voice that spoke English like the educated gentleman he was, and always, even when he went to Washington as the guest of the President, wearing a soft white Stetson. His friendships could run the gamut from Roosevelt to Calamity Jane and back again without stumbling. That was the West and Seth Bullock.

One of my early vivid memories of my father is like a long rainy day with clouds tearing themselves to shreds along the cañon walls and then, late in the afternoon, a gorgeous rainbow arched over the tops of the pine trees. It began in the early evening in the lamp-lit back parlor. Mother sat beside the hard-coal burner rocking her baby while Father

A Deadwood Judge

walked up and down into the shadowy front parlor and back again, and talked to her. The rest of us were little and nobody paid any attention to us, but I never forgot what he said. He was running for Congress then and he was telling her how the campaign was going. He seemed to be very low in his mind about it.

The fire light threw a ruddy glow on the glass doors of the big bookcase. When Father, his hands behind him and his head down, walked into its red circle of light, the world seemed to brighten a little, and then the light went low as his tall figure merged into the shadows of the unlighted room.

"I won't be elected," he said, his voice coming ahead of him as he turned at the bay window and came back toward us. "I won't get it. I never got anything in my life that I wanted so much."

It seemed to me that if I had been Mother, I would have resented that a little. He got her, and certainly from all I had heard and seen in my association with them, he had wanted her and always been glad that he got her. But she seemed to understand that this was something different, and she tried futilely to cheer him up.

"Those fellows on the other side of the river," he said, without finishing the sentence. It was always from the other side of the river that all the trouble for the Black Hills came. There was only one river in the world so far as Black Hillers were concerned. It flowed dark and treacherous on the other side of the Sioux reservation, cutting first the territory of Dakota and then the state of South Dakota, into hostile, nonunderstanding halves. "The other side

55

of the river," was farther away from us both in sympathy and transportation than Wyoming, Colorado, Nebraska, or Montana. It was peopled, I thought, with a race of horned villains whose one purpose in life was to destroy the Black Hills, from Bear Butte to Devil's Tower, from the Cheyenne River to the Belle Fourche, and from the bottom of the Homestake mine to the top of Harney Peak. That was all they lived for. Of course, they would defeat Father for Congress. They wouldn't let anybody from the Black Hills have anything.

I went about during the remaining weeks of that campaign draped in a heavy cloak of gloom. I couldn't stand seeing my father as disappointed as he was going to be when the returns came in. Nobody noticed my sadness or anything else about me except when my anxiety now and then expressed itself in a burst of temper, and then my mother told me reprovingly that "this was no time to show how disagreeable I could be." I forced my gloom on Halle until she firmly believed there would be "bears and earthquakes peeking in the window and red devils running through the house." She asked Mother about it and came back and told me things weren't as bad as I thought.

On election night Father and the General stayed down town. They didn't come home to dinner and we had no telephone in those days. They were not inconsiderate of Mother. They simply could not leave the center of things and they had no way of getting word to her. We sat around the fire in excited suspense. We'd have to hear something from somebody sometime. Mother

A Deadwood Judge

thought they must know by now. Even the "other side of the river" was at the end of a telegraph line and the territory was too sparsely populated to make the counting of ballots a lengthy affair.

Suddenly we heard the sound of a horse's slowing hoof-beats. "That's the paper," Mother said in a tense low voice. "Run out quick, Estelline, and get it."

The newsboy leaned down from his saddle to give me the paper and the verbal news, "Well, little girl, your father's elected."

I fairly flung the paper in my mother's lap. "He's 'lected."

I sat down on a little stool behind the stove and cried.

"What you crying for?" Halle asked in disgust. Her little pink-cheeked face was radiant.

"Don't be silly," Mother added, but she spoke gently and smiled. There was a suspicion of moisture in her own eyes.

He had won it, the thing he wanted so much he was sure he couldn't have it.

It was not long after we came home from Washington, all of us with a little more *savoir faire,* a little smattering of knowledge about a world outside a gold camp in a deep, narrow gulch, that I remember walking down town with Father one Sunday afternoon. He wore a Prince Albert coat as usual and a high silk hat. He wore the hat carelessly and thought nothing about it. I looked at him out of the corner of my eye now and then as we walked along Williams street and down the Lee street steps and hoped that everyone who saw us knew he was my father. Of course, most of them did. I was sure he was the handsomest man that ever lived. I liked the straight line of his nose and the firm cut of his chin and his mouth under the jet-black mustache. He was over six feet tall and he looked distinguished as well as handsome. I remembered what my Aunt Mary, his sister just younger than he, had told me once about how she used to sit in church and look around to see if there was another boy as handsome as her brother and there never was. We always have had a great deal in common, Aunt Mary and I.

At the bank corner at the foot of the steps we passed Frank Bryant, an old pioneer and prospector. At the post office we met several of Father's friends. We got the mail that had come in on the belated stagecoach while we were at dinner and was at least five days old and then we came home, up the slant of Shine street and around the corner by the Methodist Church. It seemed a very harmless little jaunt for a dignified gentleman to take with his young daughter. But the next night at dinner the General brought him a message that carried the force of an ultimatum.

"Frank Bryant told me to tell you," in a voice that carried deep sympathy with the sender of the message, "that it was bad enough to have to put up with the clothes and manners of tenderfeet. After all, they don't know any better. But when an old-timer like Judge Bennett—a regular Westener—comes along wearing a stovepipe, it's more than Deadwood Gulch can stand. Something's got to be done about it. All the traditions of the West are threatened."

A Deadwood Judge

Father smiled a little and said nothing. But he never wore his silk hat again.

It was his soft black Stetson that he lifted courteously a few days later to one of the most notorious women of the town as was his wont whenever he chanced to pass her on the street. He was walking across town with another man when they met her.

"Good morning, Miss Grace," Father said pleasantly as he lifted his hat.

The other man looked straight ahead until she had passed and then at Father in amazement. "Do you speak to that woman?" he asked, not crediting the evidence of his own eyes and ears.

"Yes," Father answered; "I can afford to." That was all.

The men who lived through the Black Hills' 'seventies built for themselves solid reputations of one sort or another on which they could stand firmly the rest of their lives. It was Father's pride that his was such that he could speak to whom he pleased and do as he liked without any sinister wonderings. Men might be astonished at things he did and people he spoke to, but they never misunderstood. An outstanding quality of those men of the 'seventies was their impregnable dignity. Especially was this true of the legal profession. Close friends and comrades though they were, they never called each other by their given names. Most of them had titles. Hank Wright was a distinctive character in my father's life because he was the only man in the Black Hills who ever called him "Granville." He was a pioneer newspaper writer of unusual ability, I remember him as a rather elderly man wearing

59

a long loose cloak instead of an overcoat, and a soft black hat that was not a Stetson. Father, who was younger than he, liked his dignified, "Good morning, Granville." He made the most of the stately name that, even though it rarely was used, suited my father so perfectly.

Yes, Deadwood's stirring 'seventies brought out the caliber of men. They were years that called for stern strength and courage. There was no way for men of flimsy mettle to reach the free, young town. The wildness and danger began with the first jack pines that stepped out along the road to meet the incoming stage or covered wagon, and the first rocky foothills that gave shelter to men whose business demanded hiding places.

Less than a month after the Black Hills were legally opened to white men the first road agents slunk out from behind a dark clump of pines and staged their first holdup within two miles of Deadwood. The stagecoach, crippled and belated by a slight accident, was lumbering in late at night, driver, messenger, and passengers all perked up and forgetting their hunger and weariness because of the lights of Deadwood that would begin to twinkle around the next bend with promises of supper, warmth, and rest.

Suddenly out of the midnight dark at the mouth of Gold Run five masked men appeared like vague black shadows. The first shot killed the driver, Johnny Slaughter, who tumbled from his high seat so easily that the messenger sitting beside him thought he had recklessly stepped down into the fray. The ensuing gun battle so terrified the horses

A Deadwood Judge

that they broke into a wild run, tangled up their harness, and brought the coach and passengers, disheveled and frightened, but safe, into Deadwood about midnight. The new sheriff, Seth Bullock, took two men and went in search. They found the body of the driver lying in the road where he had fallen, with a circle of thirteen buckshot over his heart.

They never found that particular gang of road agents but Sheriff Bullock's search for them was such that he scared them out of his county. They never came near Deadwood again but they harassed the Deadwood coach at a safer distance from Seth Bullock's keen eye and quick trigger.

The Cold Springs Cañon robbery in 1878 is one of the most famous in Black Hills history because it was the one time the treasure coach—a traveling vault with an armed guard—ever was attacked. The treasure coach, built especially for carrying Black Hills gold bullion to the railroad on its way to the mint, was lined with heavy steel plate and carried, besides the regular messenger—the courier of the stage—an extra armed guard. It made the journey several times between Deadwood and Sidney, Nebraska, with its precious load of bullion with the six-shooters lying across the knees of the guards unneeded all the way until the day it drew up to the fancied security of the Cold Springs Cañon stage station.

It was a wild, remote location at the head of a deep, heavily-timbered cañon. All around it the mountains rose thick with pines. The only approach was along the stage road. Yet one man stayed there alone and unafraid to tend the horses and take care of the station business. He was sitting on a bench in front of the log stable, in one corner of which he had his living quarters, reading an old magazine a stagecoach passenger had given him, when a stranger came around the corner of the stable and asked for a drink of water. When the stock tender came back with a dipper full of water, he faced the barrel of a six-shooter.

Half an hour later the treasure coach pulled up in front of the station. Big 'Gene was on the box driving; Scott Davis, chief messenger sat beside him; and Gale Hill, a messenger, and two other men were inside with the gold. Everything around the station was quiet—alarmingly quiet. 'Gene had thrown his lines to the ground and was preparing to dismount. There was no rattle of harness or stamping of horses, no friendly greeting from the lonely stock tender. As Big 'Gene threw his ribbons to the ground, he was met by a fusillade of bullets. One of the men in the coach was killed. Gale Hill received wounds from which he died in Deadwood several years later. Scott Davis made for the timber and fired so fast and furiously that the road agents took Big 'Gene, whom they had captured and disarmed, and using him as a shield, stopped Davis' firing. Then they compelled the driver to take a pick and open the treasure box and, appropriating the $45,000 worth of gold bullion, mounted their horses and rode away. Inside the station the stock tender was found bound and gagged. On the floor of the coach a third messenger who had been playing dead, came to life, and a road agent lying wounded in the road, was so

A Deadwood Judge

infuriated at his comrades for leaving him to his fate, that he told their names and their haunts, information that made it possible to capture most of them, send them promptly to the penitentiary, and recover the greater part of the bullion. After that the treasure coach went its way in safety.

Back and forth over those hazardous roads my father traveled several times a year. He went by all the various routes—Sidney, Bismarck, Pierre, at all times of the year, and he never saw a road agent. He heard wild tales of them along the way. He knew about that first bold holdup under the very shadow of the law he had just brought into Deadwood. He knew of the famous Cold Springs Cañon robbery and dozens of others. Many road agents were tried before him and sentenced to prison. He knew that the narrow gulches and dark places along the stage ways were full of them and their sure, wicked guns. The coach ahead of him was held up more than once and he and his fellow passengers came into meal stations to hear the thrilling details of what they narrowly had missed. Travelers in the coach that followed his had climbed out at the behest of the masked gentlemen and held up their hands while their pockets and boots and hats were rifled. But the stagecoach in which Father traveled trundled along over the perilous paths as safely as though it had been wending its way through a quiet lane in a peaceful countryside.

Once, long years after, when the railroads were running into the Hills and the country was all settled and safe, Father met a reformed road agent down at Rapid City and talked to him about those old days.

Old Deadwood Days

"It's strange," Father said, "that I never was in a holdup. I traveled in and out a great deal and I never saw any of you. I've always thought it was very curious."

The reformed road agent laughed. "No, Judge," he said, "that wasn't strange and it wasn't an accident. We always knew what stage you were on and we wouldn't take any chances of having you recognize us if we got caught and were brought up before you. The safest place in the world from road agents was always in the coach with you."

On the Long, Long Trails

Chapter 3

ON THE LONG, LONG TRAILS

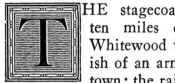HE stagecoach was dashing up the ten miles of mountain road from Whitewood with the triumphant flourish of an army that has taken a walled town; the railroad was watching Deadwood with a purposeful eye from its last stronghold in the foothills and appraising the curves, tunnels, and heavy grades that lay between; when a few stage drivers and messengers disentangled themselves from the colorful crowd and stood alone, their white Stetsons halos of a romantic past.

I had known many stage drivers casually when I was a little girl. I had ridden with them on the high box seat of the coach—first between the driver and my father who talked of wild adventures until every little line of willows marking the bed of an uncertain creek was a·skulking army of Sioux, and every dark little rock was a grizzly bear. As each stage station was slowly sketched out of the brown plains by the narrowing distance, I expected to find the long low cabins deserted and adorned with rows of bloody scalps while red men in war paint danced, and white men in black masks waited behind the log walls to spring out and add us to their bloody clutter of silent victims.

I had the personnel of the enemy darkly confused

in those early days. Indians and road agents were alike to me—wild men who lived only to devour stagecoaches and their occupants, giant ogres in enchanted forests. Drivers, messengers, and fathers were the demigods who circumvented their evil plans and saved the race of Westerners from annihilation. When I was old enough to differentiate I cut them very sharply into two classes—the robbed and resentful wards of the nation, one-time owners of all the West; and the outcast white men who had never owned nor earned an ounce of gold dust or an hundredth interest in a staked-out claim—men who would rather hide their cowardly faces behind masks, and jump out from behind trees to shoot, and take the chance of being shot, than dig for gold, learn a profession, drive horses, or 'tend bar. There was a very clear distinction between the two bands of marauders.

Those who never have lived and regulated their lives by the *crescendo* and *diminuendo* rumble of a stagecoach, and found in its daily coming and going their one excitement, their one far glimpse of another world, cannot understand the disaster of missing it for several days at a time. Even to those of us who lived in a lively camp surrounded by sociable, friendly people, the daily arrival and departure of the stagecoach were important events— the high lights of the day. The stagecoach was more intimate than a railroad train. It had fewer and smaller interests of its own. Deadwood was the most important town in the world to the stagecoach. It was the only one on the long stage trail that saw it dressed up in its six horses, nickel-plated trappings, and spectacular manners. Four horses, ordinary harness, and unostentatious driving were good enough not only for the towns along the way but for the other terminus that was out on the river or the railroad.

The stagecoach came into Deadwood and went out dashing, prancing, rolling, and glittering. Its canvas curtains might be shabby and dirty, its wheels ragged with the gumbo mud of the badlands, but it always was a romantic valiant courier to and from the outside world. Days that the stage did not arrive were days of harrowing suspense in this isolated island of mountains in a sea of flat Indian reservations. We were lost if it failed us, and sometimes men were sent out on horseback to search for it.

Often when the weather was stormy and the gumbo deep, we were a week or more without a stagecoach. We might as well have been camped on the edge of Mars. Its rumbling heard for a distance of a mile or more was as distinctive and unmistakable as gold.

Experienced miners are sometimes fooled by something that looks like gold. But gold itself is as sure as sunlight. When it strings around the bottom of the pan or winks out from a bit of quartz, the veriest tenderfoot knows it is gold. None of us ever mistook any other down-gulch noise for the rumble of the coach.

I scarcely had achieved the dignity of my 'teens when I was permitted occasionally on a straight level space, with a dependable quartet of horses and close supervision, to handle the complicated ribbons. I thought I was a highly proficient horsewoman, competent to drive any four-horse team anywhere. I know now that the driver beside me never was as casual as he seemed. I know that he never took his eyes off the eight alert ears before us and the ragged, fluted, brown road ahead. I know that no matter how absorbing the tale might be that he was telling, his skillful hands never were more than a quarter of a second away from the lines I held.

I built up in those days a strong, lasting friendship for the craft. All stage drivers had in common certain qualities that aroused my affectionate admiration. They had a high courage that mocked at danger. They had no concern at all about the terror that stalked behind trees and rocks and little hills. It was all a part of the scenery even when it moved and pulled a gun.

Whatever of glamour and romance has been left to circle around the heads of the men who "drove stage" through more than two hundred miles of dangerous loneliness, belongs to them as surely as their Stetson hats. They were afraid of nothing. Their minds clicked to a sudden crisis as quickly as their Winchesters. The hazards and hardships were accepted as a part of the day's work. They knew more about horses than Alexander the Great and they loved every one they ever drove. The long whip was just a spectacular flourish like the nickel-plated harness and the gallop into Deadwood. They never hurt their horses. They never hurled the language at them that bull-whackers did at their oxen. I spoke about this to a stage driver once and he said horses weren't dumb like oxen. They had sense. They had more than most men, and were more companionable. Any man who ever rode or drove horses successfully made friends with them. But who ever could be chummy with an ox?

The stagecoaches and the ox-drawn freight outfits followed the emigrant wagon and the pony express, but it was not until the twenty-fifth of September, 1876, that the first stagecoach rolled triumphantly into Deadwood with Dave Dickey handling the ribbons. He was an old plainsman who had served his apprenticeship on the overland route to California. Having achieved the glory of bringing the first stage successfully into Deadwood, he seemed to lose interest in the town and must have gone on to still unconquered trails. No one seems to have known him well. Captain C. V. Gardner came in on that coach as a sort of messenger, although the office and name had not yet been established. Jointly with the driver, he was responsible for the safety of the coach and the passengers. Considering the trouble that had attended all previous attempts to bring a passenger coach into Deadwood, it was no light charge. Several stagecoaches belonging to that same Gilmer and Salisbury line, trying to reach Deadwood from Cheyenne had been obliged to choose between turning back or being scalped. They all had chosen the turning back. Then apparently without any fuss or flourish, Dickey brought a stagecoach into Deadwood with all his passengers and their scalp locks intact. Having achieved this and blazed the way for all the drivers who were to follow, he drove out of the picture again.

There were scores of men on that high seat in the fourteen years between Dickey and Frank Hunter,

Old Deadwood Days

the man who drove the last stage out of Deadwood. On the Gilmer and Salisbury line that ran coaches first from Cheyenne and then from Sidney, each driver had a string of horses that he drove thirty or forty miles. On the Northwestern line from Bismarck and later from Pierre, the drivers changed with the horses every ten or twelve miles.

The men who drove the spectacular last ten miles into Deadwood were naturally the ones we knew best. One of the bright and shining stars among them was Handsome Harry whose "real" name was Hans Hansen. The General pointed him out to me one day as we stood on the corner of Main and Gold streets to watch the stage come in before we climbed the stairs to dinner. He was a big man with a heavy brown mustache, large bright blue eyes, and pink cheeks. His beauty was of the confident, obvious type. He was a showman too, wearing his white Stetson at a jaunty angle on his brown curls, and knowing how to make the most of his six prancing white horses in their nickel-plated harness, of his safely-swaying coach, his swirling whip, and his own personal beauty. On his high seat with his hands full of lines and whip he was a picture that no one ever forgot.

It was less than a year later that the General came home one night, sat down a little wearily on the front steps, and asked me if I remembered Handsome Harry. He said he had just been over to see him in his room at the Overland Hotel, that he was very sick, with mountain fever, and probably would not get well. The General felt badly about it.

"John Belding and I went over to see him," he

72

On the Long, Long Trails

said, "and tried to cheer him up, but it isn't any use. He knows." The General smiled a little crookedly. "I told him I thought he was looking better and would be out and driving again in a week or two anyway, but he just shook his head. 'No,' he said, 'I'm on the down grade and I can't reach the brake block.'"

He died sometime that night, leaving behind him, stronger and more persistent than the memory of his horsemanship, showmanship, and kindly good fellowship, the reputation of having been the handsomest man who ever came into Deadwood Gulch.

Another of the best known of the old stage drivers whose life was snuffed out long before the railroads had run their right of way across his profession was Johnny Slaughter who was killed in the first road agent holdup scarcely two miles out of Deadwood one March midnight in '77.

Despite the perils of the long trails, most drivers lived to meet the question of a substitute profession. The new order brought in by the railroad offered them little recompense for the passing of a life lived in the open with the sweep of wind across wide spaces and down the mountain side at night, the tug of mettlesome horses at their fingers' ends, and the fillip of possible danger on every horizon. To the old overland drivers, those were dull days the stagecoach left behind. They faced the change according to their different philosophies and temperaments.

Billy Welsh made himself famous by his classic request for information on a subject concerning which all men were speculating at the time. It was the day after President Garfield died. Father was

73

waiting in the office of the Wentworth Hotel to see
an eastern capitalist client who had come in on the
stage and was indulging in the three-days' neglected
luxury of shaving, when Billy Welsh came in and
drew a wooden armchair up to the stove. Father
told us about it at dinner and made Mother forget
that he was late and the steak dry and overdone.

Billy had slouched down in his chair, Father told
us, and asked of the crowd in general: "If some son
of a gun pops off this here Arthur, who'll take his
string of stock and go on?" He looked around the
circle that included eminent lawyers and experienced politicians, but no one of them could tell
him.

In the middle 'eighties when the railroad was too
close for his pleasure, Billy left the Hills and won
further fame by fighting a duel with a miner up in
Idaho. He came out of the affair of honor, whatever its genesis, unharmed, and didn't hurt the other
fellow much. The last heard of him was from New
Mexico where he had a little stage line of his own
and was working his own string of stock over a
twelve-mile run.

Fred Doten, wiry, gray-eyed, typically western,
graduated from the long stagecoach trail to a hack
between Deadwood and the up-gulch towns. It was
one of the familiar high "standard hacks" of those
days—a barbarous vehicle with three wide spring
seats that made you wonder when you finally got in
and sat down why you had taken so much trouble to
arrive at so much discomfort. You stepped up onto
the hub of the wheel and then climbed laboriously
over the accumulated mud of many previous trips,

On the Long, Long Trails

and went some place that you had to go. You didn't take a pleasure trip in a standard hack. Fred, in common with every other man who had driven six horses as a business, mourned for the old days. He found the hack and the two amiable horses trotting along the friendly roadways very tame and stupid. It took a driver to drive six horses over rough roads that hugged a mountain wall. Even four horses on the plains and in the foothills in troublous times required some skill. A child could drive two horses to Lead and Golden Gate. Yet Fred readjusted his care-free life with amazing ease. He was blithe and alert on his semihigh seat and his conversation, unless deliberately diverted, ran along the way of current living. Later he was elected sheriff, married, and seemed fairly reconciled to a safe conservative life.

Harvey Fellows came down from the driver's seat of the overland stagecoach and climbed directly up on the box of the Spearfish stage where he made friends with all the boys and girls who went from the Hills towns out to the Spearfish Normal School.

Among other drivers, memory of whom is most persistent among the pioneers, were Russ Hawley who laid down his reins to go to work for the Homestake mining company, Big 'Gene Barnett who was driving the treasure coach at the time of the Cold Springs Cañon holdup, Hank Monk, Bob Pugh, Red Raymond, Paul Clinton, Wally Walker, Dan Callahan, Jim Madden, and Kid Walker.

George Gates who taught me to drive was slim, and dark with sleepy, sloe-black eyes. He slouched in the low seat of the old-fashioned two-seated carriage that served as one of the hacks between Deadwood and up-gulch and seemed to be paying no attention at all to his horses or to the road. Just so, I am sure, he might have driven through the hostile Indian country in '76 and the treacherous cañon ways around the Hat Creek and Cold Springs stage stations in '77 when the knights of the road behind black masks and big guns slipped rudely out of hiding and crashed the most peaceful bits of driving. He seemed utterly indolent and indifferent, but from under the brim of his soft white hat, he saw every track in the road, every flick of his horses' ears. He talked in a soft, drawling voice to any passenger who rode beside him, but he heard each hoof beat and every rattle of unseen wheels on the cramped highway. He never was caught unprepared in one of the numerous stretches of road where teams could not pass.

"Keep away from the edge of the road," he would admonish me when the drop into Gold Run was not more than two or three gently falling feet. "Get the habit of hugging the hill. The time to drive on the edge of a precipice is when there's no place else to drive. There's nothing smart about seeing how near you can come to going over."

He himself could, I am sure, have driven six prancing steeds over a high-strung slack wire. When the little narrow-gauge road that tipped up from Deadwood to Lead put even the hacks out of business, he joined the gold rush to Alaska.

In addition to their skill in driving, and their alertness in distinguishing feathered heads and

On the Long, Long Trails

masked faces farther than most people could see a mountain range, the old stage drivers were *raconteurs* of no light ability. It was as much a part of the driver's business to entertain the tenderfoot on the box beside him as it was to drive his horses with light, sure hand and sense what was happening over the horizon. Some acquired reputations as storytellers that have settled down with them beside their peaceful firesides in the Hills.

Chief among these is Chris Jensen who, as the railroad approached the foothills from the south, owned his own stage lines between the Hills towns. His story of an encounter with Indians is part of the folklore of the Black Hills. He told it first to a couple of school teachers coming out on their initial trip in the early 'eighties with such glittering success that he kept it in his *repertoire* for years. Thrill-weary old-timers tell it to-day with chuckles of glee, and I, squeezed in between the teachers, heard that first telling.

"You've been driving stage quite a while now, haven't you, Mr. Jensen?" one of the school teachers had preambled.

Chris admitted that he had. Five or six years was a long time in the Black Hills in the 'eighties. There was no great span of time to look back over.

"You must have had some exciting experiences," the other teacher hazarded.

Yes, he agreed, it was not always a quiet little afternoon pleasure drive. He had had his crowded moments. He had met road agents and Indians. A man couldn't drive every day for months and years without running into some rough traveling.

"Tell us about it," the teachers urged in unison. "Do tell us about an experience with Indians."

Chris had told his Indian stories over until he was tired of them. He had told some on this trip. But the ladies were insistent and so he began on a perfectly new story.

"Well," he said with seeming reluctance, "here's one I don't often tell."

That was the story they wanted.

"We was drivin' along in the foothills," he began, "and we was lucky. We hadn't seen a sign of an Injun. Then, just as we come up on a narrow piece of road along a steep hillside with a deep gorge on one side and a wall of rock on the other, they were in front of us. We couldn't tell how many. The road was plumb crammed with 'em around the curve just beyond. They were all in war paint and feathers with their bows and arrows drawed. I pulled my gun but they let fly first and one of the front horses reared up and rolled down the hill. He'd have taken us all with him only the harness broke. But I was thrown off the box and my gun follered after the horse. By the time I picked myself up and was reaching for my other gun in the boot, the other horse broke and run. There were half a dozen passengers and they spilled out in various places but they all got away safe somewhere except one that was killed in the beginning. I was alone on that little shelf of a road with Indians in front of me, and a bunch of them that had sneaked up behind me from somewhere and no way out on either side until I saw a little opening in the rock wall. If I could get there and make the top through

On the Long, Long Trails

that ragged ledge I might get down into the timber on the other side and lose the red devils. I edged my way up slinking behind young pines when I could and finally with a few arrows sticking in me, I got to the top of the mountain with all the Injuns pressin' close behind me. The other side was just as bare as the one I'd climbed and there, crawlin' up from the lower slopes were about a thousand more Injuns. The mountain side was red with 'em. I fired the last shot I had out of the old six-shooter, and they were so close I could have picked an eagle feather out of any one of their war bonnets.

"I was all alone on the bare top of the mountain without a shot in my gun and them painted devils crawling closer every minute."

Chris paused for a brief moment. "Yes, yes," one of the school teachers gasped. "And what did you do then, Mr. Jensen? What did you do?"

He let his little pause grow dramatic and then, casually and a little sadly: "I died."

A soft south wind moaned through the pine trees. The four horses slowed their easy trot to a funeral march, and the rattle of the stagecoach diminuendoed gently.

"Yes," Chris resumed in low voice for the finale, "they killed me. I'm buried over there in that clump of tall pines on the other side of the cañon."

Down the road ahead of us the stage station came into view. Chris let out his "Yip-yip-yip-yip-yi-yi-yi-yi" and from somewhere in the barn the stocktender appeared with his horses harnessed and ready. In the confusion of arrival, the medley of voices, and tramp of hoofs as the old horses were led out of the traces and the new ones hitched up, Chris climbed down from the box and disappeared. It was the end of his run.

Mother wanted to know what I was giggling about when I got in beside her but I couldn't tell her because the teachers had come, too. No one told them about the real tragedy at this station we were just leaving. Probably they wouldn't have listened. The Spring Valley murder was something that really had happened.

Spring Valley was no different from the other stage stations. They all were lonely and monotonous. The ten miles between them were longer than a hundred miles to-day and the two stagecoaches going in opposite directions, that stopped to change horses and sometimes for meals, were the only events of the twenty-four hours. Long bull-trains dragged past, and occasionally in the earliest years an emigrant train. If the weather was harsh and the roads heavy, there might be days or even weeks when the stock-tender and his helper and his wife, if he had one, saw nobody but one another. One roof covered the stable and the living quarters. If the stock-tender and his helper lived alone they had a little room partitioned off from the stable. At the meal stations and wherever there was a woman, the accommodations were a little more elaborate and comfortable. Living rooms did not open directly into the horses' apartments and there might be two rooms instead of one.

The Spring Valley station, when we had driven up there one day the winter before, had looked no different from the others, no different from this day

On the Long, Long Trails

when it served as an opportune period to Chris Jensen's tale of adventure. That had been a bitter cold day and ours was the first coach to get through in three days. We should have changed horses there and had dinner. We had come long, hungry miles since an early breakfast and it was the middle of the afternoon when we saw the Spring Valley station crawling slowly toward us. The driver's heralding call brought no sign of life as we drove up. There should have been two men there, Adler and Garver, but there was no sign of either. As the driver pulled his horses to a stop, he called again and a big blond woman came out. She said something in a whisper to the messenger who had climbed down. He called to Father and they went aside to talk to her. Pretty soon the messenger and the woman went into the house and Father came back to the coach. Listening intently, I heard him tell the driver that he was to drive on to Jack Hale's. Hard as I tried I could not hear what else he said. When he got into the coach Father said we would get something to eat at Jack Hale's horse ranch and we started on. The messenger stayed behind, an unheard of thing for a messenger to do. Even I knew that.

A fat man was the only other passenger on the coach and he and Mother only looked at Father and asked him nothing. Halle and Robbie and I fussed a little about food but Father spoke sternly to us. He said a delayed meal was a matter of no consequence whatever compared with some other things, and vaguely I sensed that the "some other things" were hiding darkly back in the Spring Valley ranch house.

Old Deadwood Days

Inadvertently the next night at home I heard Father telling the General about the Spring Valley tragedy.

"The big blond woman," he said, "who was handsome in a rough, buxom sort of way, had been living with Adler and helping with the cooking. They had been unable to get out at all during the winter. Stages had been delayed so much that often for days at a time they had seen no one but each other and often their supplies ran low. Toward the end of the winter each one was in a temper for trouble. Adler developed a slow, unreasoning jealousy of Garver that worked itself up in the dull, cloudy cold until, the night before we arrived, when no one had been past the station for three days, he shot and killed him.

"Adler was still in the house. He had not tried to get away. He couldn't have done it anyway in that weather but he was intending to plead self-defense."

By the time the sheriff brought them to Deadwood the woman had turned against Adler. Obviously she didn't want to be mixed up in his end of the tragedy. I heard a good deal about the affair because I pricked up my ears every time it was mentioned, and I read all there was in the papers about it.

The woman decided that her best play was to claim she had been Garver's wife and when a brother came out from the "States" to settle up the dead man's small affairs, she insisted upon her widow's rights. The trial of Adler and the settling up of Garver's business dragged along until the

On the Long, Long Trails

brother threatened to take matters into his own hands and put an end to Adler himself, but he never did. Nobody attached any importance at all to the woman. The General said the drivers and messengers all knew she had been "Adler's woman" and had throwed him down as soon as he got into trouble. The General always insisted that "throwed" was a western colloquialism and as such, perfectly correct. Her sort of woman could get no sympathy from western men. Eventually Adler was acquitted.

"It would have been different," Mr. Bonham said once when he was recalling the story, "if he'd stolen a horse."

When the young Homestake mining company began shipping gold bullion to the United States mint in such quantities that its transportation became a serious responsibility the old Cheyenne stage company put on a treasure coach that was a steel-lined, ironclad, portholed fort on wheels. The Northwestern company that later carried the gold bricks out, used a coach that differed from passengers coaches only in having the center seat removed and carrying no one but armed guards. The treasure was carried in heavy steel chests. The treasure coach made two trips a month, following the semi-monthly clean-ups at the mines and in the years before it turned its mission over to the railroad, the treasure coach transported nearly sixty million dollars in gold bullion. It never lost an ounce of gold. Once the gold bricks were mislaid in the Cañon Springs holdup but were recovered when the father of one of the robbers, who was a respectable banker in a little Iowa town, naïvely exhibited them in the bank window. His son had told him he had sold a mine. Some one who knew that mines were not paid for in gold bricks, saw them and notified the stage company. The bricks were recovered but the robber was not captured.

On the day of the Homestake clean-up, the gold bricks lay, shining and arrogant, and heavily guarded, in the bank window. Five bricks were brought down loose to the bank where they were wrapped in heavy canvas, sealed, and addressed. Their aggregate value varied from $95,000 to $148,000. Never in all the years that they were on exhibition regularly for a fraction of a day every fortnight, did they fail to create a sensation. After the railroad came they were taken direct to the express car and no one saw them except at the Homestake assay office where you were told that if you could lift a brick, you could have it. But once I lifted one a fraction of an inch and they did not give it to me.

The most valuable shipment ever made by treasure coach was $350,000 worth of bullion that went out one day in July, '77, the time the road agents were at their worst. Knowledge of the extraordinary shipment could not fail to reach the outlaws, and the usual guard of five armed messengers was increased to thirteen. Four were mounted, one riding in advance, one on either flank, and one in the rear of the coach at a distance of about three hundred yards. They rode on a gallop carefully reconnoitering, but not a shadow disturbed the smooth safety of the journey. At Grand River, it

TREASURE COACH AT CANYON SPRINGS

The only time the road agents succeeded in holding up the treasure coach and getting away with the gold bullion was in 1878. The gold bricks were later recovered.

(From a newspaper print of that year—1878.)

PROSPECTORS IN DEADWOOD GULCH 1876

Prospectors in 1876 outfitted at the Big Horn Store that is still doing business (1928) in the same location, under the same ownership.

(From an old photograph.)

On the Long, Long Trails

was learned later, a little band of road agents waited in hiding for the $350,000 worth of gold bullion but were routed in alarm by the sight of the unexpected cavalcade.

The last of the holdups was such a bitter disappointment to the road agents, thinned both in numbers and acumen by that time, that they faded off the trails entirely. It was one cold February night in '85 that they appeared abruptly before the driver and messenger in a lonely spot below Running Water on the Sidney route and ordered them to throw up their hands. The demand met with immediate compliance. The driver holding firmly in place with his feet the long lines he had dropped inside the dashboard, and lifting his hands high and empty toward the black sky, leaned down to the nearest road agent and requested that the affair be conducted as quietly as possible because his only passengers were two women who were asleep and who had nothing anyhow. The road agent verified this to his own satisfaction by lifting the canvas curtain lightly and looking in. Then they demanded the treasure box. The messenger reached for it with a gun pointed at his head and threw it into the underbrush. The road agents saw where it landed and allowed the stage to drive on. It was well out of reach before the box was opened and found to be entirely empty.

When Scott Davis, chief of the treasure coach messengers who began service in '77, resigned in '86, only three of the exclusive treasure messengers were left—Billy Sample, Bill Linn, and Dick Bullock. Davis wandered down into Nebraska and in 1890 some one brought back word to the Hills that he was buyer for a big horse and cattle company at Fremont, Nebraska. He must have found it very tame and quiet.

Billy Sample stayed as long as he could without waiting to see the railroad come in to Deadwood. While it still was at Whitewood he "pulled his freight," and was last heard of in Mexico City where he had a position as messenger on a Mexican Central run eight hundred miles long with twenty stations along the way.

Bill Linn who lacked only five inches of being seven feet tall and could strike terror to road agents just by standing up, stayed in Deadwood after the adventurous job was done.

Dick Bullock, one of the most intrepid among them, never forsook the Homestake gold bricks, not even after the days came when they traveled only a scant four miles from the mine to the railroad station at Deadwood. Their journey to Philadelphia then, while less spectacular, certainly was safer. There are more people around a railroad train than a stagecoach, and it's harder to catch.

Paul Blum, who was a messenger on the Bismarck route, is the only one on record who got disgusted with "the layout," and quit. After being held up on two successive runs in exactly the same place, he decided that fate and the road agents were unreasonable and betook himself to a stage from which he faced footlights and a friendly audience instead of guns and masked men. He came back to Deadwood with Grace Hawthorne's company nearly ten years later when the treasure coaches,

On the Long, Long Trails

although still carrying armed guards, went out unmolested, and passenger coaches traveled in safety and comparative comfort.

'Gene Decker had been a newspaper reporter before he started on his initial trip as messenger on the treasure coach under Scott Davis. He was resourceful and unafraid but Davis didn't know much about him and wanted to try out his mettle.

"If a road agent should pop his head up along here," he asked as the coach rumbled along through the foothills with straggling pines and gypsum cliffs ambling by on the right hand horizon, "what would you do? Shoot or get down in the boot?"

Decker answered quietly that he thought he would shoot.

"What makes you think you would shoot?" Davis persisted. "How do you know?"

"Well," Decker drawled with more impatience in his mind than in his voice or manner, "if you want to know, get down and pretend you're a road agent. We'll shoot it out right here."

Davis was satisfied without making any test. It was the newspaper business that called 'Gene Decker back from the trails. He went to Montana and later opened a curio shop in Billings.

Gail Hill, slim, young, with a boyish idealistic face, was married into the Winn family that lived in tribal unity in a row of little houses on the narrowing point of Williams street and Centennial avenue, the family living farthest from the corner having the longest lot. He received a wound at the Cañon Springs holdup from which he died several years later. I knew his children and his wife and

Old Deadwood Days

I used to see him in those early 'eighties, a youthful fragile-looking hero that I never forgot. He made the road agents a reality.

Boone May who was a mighty hunter as well as a fearless messenger brought back from one hunting trip with Captain Willard in the fall of '81, eight hundred buffalo robes. He never was overtaken by the quiet life. From the Hills he went to Bolivia and wrote back to some of his friends that he had acquired valuable mining interests there and was doing well. But the next news of him concerned some trouble with a Brazilian officer over a dark-eyed South American beauty. May had shot the officer and left for the mountains. He stayed in hiding with the Indians near the head of the Amazon until he thought the Brazilians had forgotten about him and then went over the Pampas to Rio Janeiro. From there he wrote to a friend in Deadwood that the yellow fever was bad in Rio, and no one ever heard from him again.

Howard Scott was not a messenger when I knew him. He was a mining engineer with one of the big companies. It was the sort of work he had expected when he came into the Hills. Messengering had been one of those between-time jobs common among the young men who came out to the West—young men who never idled. Bob Ogden who had known him well back in New Orleans, had told Maude Dennee and me about him. It was just before Mr. Ogden and Maude were married and we had all gone out to this picnic together, at Horseshoe grove, the park that cuddled in the timber in a curve of the Homestake wood road.

On the Long, Long Trails

"I never saw you before to-day," Mr. Scott told me as we danced, "but once I did you a little service and I heard your voice and knew who you were."

The music stopped then and we went and sat down outside the pavilion under a big pine tree and he told me about the part he had played in an unforgotten chapter in the life of our little black and tan dog, Don. It was one fall several years before when we were coming back to Deadwood from our homestead down in the cattle country between Fall River and Cheyenne, Mother, Halle, Robbie, Gaylord, myself, and Don. We had a large wagon with such household goods as we transported to and fro, a big and competent but slow team of horses, and a man to drive.

Don's inexperienced youth and his long summer on the ranch had made him a recluse and fearful of everybody and everything he didn't know and understand which was practically everything outside the family and the cabin on the ranch. Once in the early summer he had ventured to run away and go with some strangers to the village of Hot Springs, a distance of four miles. While he was there some unprincipled scoundrel, as we learned afterwards, took a shot at him. He came home at a faster pace than the bullet that had frightened him. We saw him coming down the long level stretch of road more than a mile away, a tiny, terrified black dot. He didn't stop to speak to us as he came up the hill and we rushed out to meet him to reassure him. His tail was between his legs and he was doubled into the smallest kind of a ball for speed. He scuttled under the cabin to his own bed in a safe secluded corner and dropped down panting and exhausted. We had to crawl in after him to take him food, water, and words of comfort and affection. We had trouble persuading him that it was all right to come out and he never again of his own volition left the immediate environs of the cabin. When we broke up housekeeping in the fall and started toward town, he was in a panic. He almost lost confidence in us. Didn't we know the deadly dangers that lurked in that big town of at least a dozen houses? But he couldn't stay behind and let us go so with yelping protests he sat in my lap and rode toward what he knew was murder and massacre and portentous alarms.

We stayed overnight at Hot Springs and he made a good deal of trouble which was not at all like Don. Halle and I settled him comfortably at the foot of our bed but while we slept he vanished. I don't know yet whether he jumped out of the window, or wriggled through a crack in the wall, but when we woke in the morning he was gone. Probably he thought it was futile to stay. Against such terrifying odds, he could protect neither us nor himself. Everybody hunted everywhere for him without avail and finally Mother and the driver insisted that we go on without him. We already had lost too much time. Mother tried to console us with the belief that some one would find him and keep him until we came back. Everybody knew him.

We started on the second day of our journey with tears and lamentations. Don was as much a part of our family as any one of us. Father had brought him home one night in his pocket when Gaylord

On the Long, Long Trails

was a baby and they had grown up to the advanced age of three years together.

That night we arrived about dark at a combination stage and meal station, had a sad supper and went directly to bed in a room separated from the dining room by a calico curtain that didn't reach the floor by a foot or more. There was one bed that Mother and the two little boys had, and another was made on the floor for Halle and me. She got in next the wall and cried herself to sleep about Don. I heard Mother having a good deal of trouble quieting the boys' grief but finally everybody seemed to be asleep but me. I lay there in the dark thinking about Don wandering around scared and lonesome and hungry. I knew no one had taken him in to feed and comfort him. He wouldn't let them. It wasn't that he was cross. He was just afraid, terribly afraid of strange places and strange people.

I was dozing off a little, despairing and grief-stricken, when I heard the stagecoach. It was the same unmistakable rumble that we heard on the ranch when it was rolling along over the hill by Gilbert Parker's hayfield, and at home when it still was away down the Boulder Cañon road. There was bustle and stirring about in the room outside, voices, and the clatter of dishes. I listened to the crescendo rumble of the stage driver's "Yip-yip-yip-yip-yi-yi-yi-yi." The horses came to a sudden stop right in front of the window above our bed. It sounded as if they had had no thought of stopping until they were there. They were so close I could hear their labored breathing, their pawing of the dry roadway, and the clank of their harness as they shook themselves into restful positions. I could hear the men talking outside and then the sound of their heavy boots on the dining room floor. Their cheerful voices came through the calico curtain and then one, softer, more gently modulated than the others asked:

"Is Judge Bennett's family here? I have the children's little dog."

I turned over and raised up on my elbow. In the space below the abbreviated curtain I saw the familiar slim black legs and small tan feet.

"Come, Don," I called softly, not to waken the family, and he came and climbed in between Halle and me and lay down with a little sigh of relief. She woke up and spoke to him too and I felt his tail wag wearily against my knee. We didn't need to watch him any more. He had come home, and home henceforth was not a place but his own people.

The slowest line across the long, long trails was made by the ox-drawn freight wagons. They dragged up the grade and into Deadwood at the deliberate pace that sometimes made the two hundred miles from the railroad a two and three months' journey. The oxen, unlike the stage horses, knew no difference between the empty plains and the peopled camp. Wagon bosses and bull-whackers made their entry into the famous town indifferently. But they came in great numbers, for Deadwood was the distributing point for all the Black Hills. Even with favorable weather the journey was too long for perishable goods. Fruit and green vegetables came through at great risk and consequently commanded

On the Long, Long Trails

enormous prices. Nothing of the sort was raised in the Hills. The 'eighties were pretty well grown before truck gardens and one or two orchards began to send in their hard-coaxed products. Potatoes and gold do not seem to flourish in the same soil. Apples arrived in the winter frozen solid and the cheerful, resourceful merchants of Deadwood forthwith made them into cider. I can't remember that it was in any way inferior to any other cider but we may not have noticed. We were neither captious nor critical in those days. We received freight gratefully, knowing the labor behind its coming. There were days in the far-out foothills and on the plains when the bull-whackers had to stop their trains and build fires around which they and their oxen huddled away from the blizzards. Who cared then whether the safely sheltered people of the Hills had apples or potatoes?

The narrow streets were jammed most of the time with the stubborn beasts and their long wagon trains. They made driving on Main and Sherman streets and their connecting arteries frequently difficult and sometimes impossible. They never ceased to be a source of interest to us. From our front steps we could see them crawl past Wall street, the number of yoke of oxen on each train varying from eight to twelve, but usually numbering ten with three wagons behind—the lead, the swing, and the trailer. The oxen in the lead yoke were the only ones that had names and that ever were addressed directly. One bull-whacker called his "Beecher" and "Tilden" and from way up on our steps we could hear him shouting: "Gee, Beecher; Gee-ee-eee, Tilden," followed

Old Deadwood Days

by a string of wicked words that flung themselves back and forth between Forest Hill and White Rocks. Sometimes when the whole gulch was so full of freight outfits that you couldn't have squeezed an ill-nourished calf in between them, two or three specially stupid yoke of oxen would get their feet over the chains and tangle up the whole train so that all traffic was stopped from Chinatown to the Congregational Church.

Sometimes a bull-whacker gave an exhibition on Main street with his long whip that was a fascinating show if you were well out of the way. I remember one particularly that I watched from the window of Goldberg's Big Horn grocery store where I had been sent on a hurried errand for sugar. I found refuge just in time. As far as his loaded lash could reach, the street, the sidewalks, and the air above belonged to the bull-whacker and his act. Mr. Goldberg said it was a marvelous whip. The man had shown it to him. Its hickory handle was four feet long, the length of the lash was one hundred feet and it was tipped with dynamite cartridges for crackers. Once in every two or three seconds he planted himself firmly in the middle of his domain, twirled the lash gracefully around his head, threw it out in the direction of the Merchants Hotel, and achieved an explosion that awoke old echoes slumbering peacefully since a geological revolution threw White Rocks up above the gulch. The populace crowded itself at safe distances and watched him admiringly. His oxen closed their eyes and chewed their cuds contentedly.

I had little opportunity to know bull-whackers

On the Long, Long Trails

personally, but three of them stand out distinctly in my memory. They were "Shorty," "Madame Canutson," and the "Harvard Man."

Everybody knew Shorty. We were coming in on the Pierre stage when I saw him for the first time. A broken axle or something of the sort had delayed us at a lonesome station and I was standing with Father watching the repairs on the stage when the bull train came along and Shorty stepped over and spoke to us. He and Father seemed to be old friends. Shorty was an ordinary sized man from his waist up but his bowed legs would have been way under length even if they had been straightened out.

"Hello, little girl," he said patting me on the head. "My legs are pretty short, ain't they?"

I was too embarrassed to answer and he went on to explain that he had "walked 'em off whackin' bulls between Pierre and Deadwood." Then he called Father's attention to a lighter train pulling out of a shallow ditch on the other side of the road. He said he had gone ahead of his train and when this one came along the wagon-boss, seeing him standing in the middle of the road and not knowing him, had made that "d——n funny detour." The oxen had objected a little. They never liked having their even slow routine interrupted. The wagon-boss came up just then and he and Shorty looked at each other in surprise.

"What did you do that for?" Shorty asked.

The other man looked down at Shorty's little bowed legs and his heavily booted feet planted firmly on the smooth level roadway, and grinned.

"I thought you was standing in a hole," he explained, and went back to his disgusted oxen.

"He'll never hear the last of that," Father commented.

"No," Shorty agreed, "it's worse than the way we got took in once back in '77 by that girl, Mollie. Did you see her, Judge?"

Father knew nothing about the girl, Mollie.

"She came to the wagon-boss at Bismarck," Shorty began, his voice expressing the several-years-old chagrin, "and asked if she could shove through with us. She had her own hoss and would just ride along with our outfit for safety and she said she could help with the cookin'. The wagon-boss thought that would be all right enough. He supposed she had a sidesaddle and would ride like a lady. He forgot all about her, and we were all so busy getting off that nobody noticed her till we were so far out he couldn't send her back. And here she was a-ridin' *à la* clothespin."

They were all shocked and horrified. They had been ashamed to come into Deadwood with her—those rough, profane bull-whackers.

Shorty and I always were friends after that and spoke to each other on the street, but I never happened to talk with him again.

And then I met Madame Canutson. We were coming home from school one glorious late fall day, Irene and Halle and I and half a dozen more little Forest Hill girls and, having instructions to come home around by the Methodist Church and not by way of Main street, we all stopped on the corner by the Wentworth Hotel and looked down to see what

On the Long, Long Trails

might be doing in the lively forbidden end of the gulch. An ox team was ambling along taking up all the street but being peaceful and quiet and making no trouble, when suddenly the head bull-whacker stopped them and dashed back past the lead and swing wagons to the trailer. A crowd assembled at once. Something interesting had happened and no one could expect us to remember any morning admonitions. By the time we reached the trailer the curious mob had thinned enough to let us into the front row. A woman in a man's clothes—we could see now that the head bull-whacker really was a bull-whackeress—was comforting a baby not more than a year old. I wondered if she talked that way when she was whacking bulls, and if she did could the bulls understand that soft, cooing language? She looked around and smiled at George Ayers who had come out of his hardware store to see what the trouble was.

"No," she said in answer to his question, "the baby ain't hurt. He tried to climb out and fell." She laughed a little. "Here he's come all the way from Pierre, more'n six weeks we've been on the way and not a thing happened to him till we get clean into Deadwood, and then he has to go an' fall out o' the wagon." She looked up at Mr. Ayers again with a mischievous smile. "He's been sleepin' in the oven of that big hotel range I'm bringin' in for you," she said. "I fixed him an awful tony bed in there."

The General came along just then and Halle and I went away with him but not until after he had spoken to the bull-whackeress. "How do you do,

Old Deadwood Days

Madame Canutson," he greeted her. It seems every-body, other freighters, all the bull-whackers, and everybody, all called her Madame Canutson.

"The little fellow is not hurt?"

"No, just a little bump on his head. He's all right now." The baby grinned in corroboration.

It was her own ox train, the General said, and she drove her ten yoke of oxen back and forth between Pierre and Deadwood with a skill that elicited admiration from the most experienced and expert bull-whackers. She kept the baby with her while her husband worked on the homestead they were proving up on out in the valley. She couldn't do the heavy work of a ranch but she could whack bulls. She rarely had to take care of her own stock. Some kindly bull-whacker did that for her.

"Does she talk to the bulls the same way she does to the baby?" I asked the General, being still curious about that in view of all I'd heard about the only language bulls could understand.

The General smiled. "Well, the bull-whackers say she doesn't. They say her vocabulary is equal to the best of them."

She had begun by night-herding, he said. Then she drove oxen, and now she had a train of her own. A smart woman!

The long leisurely journey across the plains with its tentative promise and occasional flash of adventure attracted men of varying caliber and background. Father who always was glad to talk to anyone from whom he could learn anything about some unknown country or phase of life, came home to dinner one night full of interest in a long conver-

98

On the Long, Long Trails

sation he had been having with a bull-whacker who was a graduate of Harvard. The man had gone to freighting for his health and to gain a knowledge of the rough side of life. He had achieved both in full measure.

Father had learned more about freighting from that young man than he ever had known in all the years he had been traveling the same trails with the bull teams and watching them bring their heavy loads slowly into Deadwood. He said that the Harvard youth's trained mind saw the bull-freighting business as a picturesque phase in the building of the West. He was more interested in that than he was in the number of pounds of freight that one ten-yoke train of oxen could haul or the number of days required to do it in between the river and the Hills. He saw the eight trains, each one with its string of oxen, its big wagon, swing, and trail, as a part of the long empire-building procession. He saw the night-herders driving in the cattle in the cool of the morning to be yoked up and driven on, the bull-whackers with their long cracking whips and lurid language, as important figures in the world-old western march of civilization. They wondered together, Father and the Harvard bull-whacker, what was going to happen when there was no more West, when the last sunset-trending trail's end ran into the open gate of the Orient.

The Harvard bull-whacker said that when the men and their beasts all stopped to rest during the long nooning, when the sun beat down on the broad plains, brown with cured buffalo grass, he was reminded of Old Testament pictures, and stories of

Old Deadwood Days

dignified nomad tribes. Oxen refused to be hurried and they did a tremendous amount of work when they were permitted to do it in their own time and way. Perhaps they were not as dumb and driven as Longfellow thought they were.

He liked night-herding best. Men on the night herd rode ponies around through the night to see that the oxen did not get restless and lose their sleep, and counted time by the stars. They slept by day, making their beds on the freight in the wagons where they could. They were not jolted hard at a pace of twelve miles a day. Of course a man made only thirty dollars a month but that was clear. In addition to his moving bed and his transportation to the Hills, he had bacon, coffee, flapjacks, and beans, free, abundant, and regularly.

He was an interesting young man, Father said, and the next time he saw him he was going to bring him home to dinner. But he never saw him again and not knowing his name, he couldn't find out much about him. He asked his friend, Fred Evans, who owned a string of freight outfits, but Mr. Evans said he had run across several college men who had taken that way of going West.

Mr. Evans, whose bull trains trailed across the Sioux reservation between the Missouri River and Deadwood for years, not only could whack bulls himself but he could, when necessary, speak their language. Once he was persuading some stubborn oxen against their inclination into Whoop-up's corral, while his good friend, the Rev. James Williams, pastor of the Methodist Church, waited for him. Fred Evans had a high regard for the profession

100

WOMAN "BULL-WHACKER" FREIGHTING TO DEADWOOD, 1876.

WOMAN "BULL-WHACKER" IN DEADWOOD, 1876.

Madame Canutson was the only "bull-whackeress" who ever drove her own bull train into Deadwood.

(Contemporary photograph of her arrival.)

PLACER MINING—DEADWOOD GULCH, 1876.

PLACER MINING IN DEADWOOD GULCH, 1876.

Deadwood Gulch made poor men rich in 1876. Placer mining required no expensive equipment and often yielded large returns.

(Contemporary photograph of the gold rush.)

On the Long, Long Trails

Mr. Williams represented. Also he guarded jealously his own position as an original charter member of the stagecoach aristocracy of the Black Hills. But he believed with the men who whacked bulls for him across the plains, that the language understood by oxen was limited as to the number of words, and none of them were in common use in polite society. It was said of him that he "could swear an ox's horn off in two minutes." Perhaps that's what became of the long-horn cattle.

While Mr. Williams waited and the oxen took their time, Mr. Evans filled the air so full of verbal blue flame that the reverend gentleman finally felt called upon to protest.

"Mr. Evans, why are you so profane? I don't think such language is necessary."

Old Fred, as he was familiarly called, straightened up to his full six feet four and turned his attention from his cushion-pated beasts to his admonitory friend.

"Not necessary, eh? That's all you know about it. It's a soft easy job to freight a soul to the sweet pretty soon, and there's no occasion to get excited and use language in that business. But when a man whacks bulls he has to cuss at them. They wouldn't understand *your* conversation. You think because you wear a black suit of clothes and a white necktie that you're pretty smart, but if you'll drive one yoke of oxen one day without cussin', I'll give you one thousand dollars. Now that's a straight proposition and you can either shoot or put up your gun."

It is not of record that Mr. Williams ever accepted the challenge.

Footlights of the Frontier

Chapter 4

FOOTLIGHTS OF THE FRONTIER

THE Gem Theater for nearly a quarter of century was a clangorous, tangling, insidious part of Deadwood's nightly life. The raucous tones of its ballyhooing brass-band in the street outside threaded through the pealing church bells like an obligato. They shrieked in blatant brass the interdependence of the good and bad in Deadwood Gulch. Their steady rhythm caught the strokes and held them together in a symbolic confusion of sound.

On the sidewalks and strips of terrace in front of our sheltered homes on Forest Hill, we learned to dance to the music of a band that the men of the family, privileged persons though they were, never followed into the theater—a theater famous even in a roaring mining camp for its iniquity. When it went inside at eight o'clock, muting and muffling its music, our curfew was rung.

The Langrishe Theater, at the other end of the dramatic octave with no tones or half-tones between left an unforgettable memory in Deadwood Gulch after three years of such acting as might have been offered to Puritan playgoers and metropolitan critics. Jack Langrishe and his wife are the only actors in the history of the theater who, given the

105

Old Deadwood Days

choice, preferred the mountains of the West to Broadway.

Scores of playhouses rang their curtains up and down and spilled their old-fashioned sentimental music over the dance floors and into the streets. Before the great fire of '79 that swept the gulch clear of its flimsy frame structures, Deadwood had more places of amusement than any other town of its size in the country. But it is these two sharply contrasted theaters, the Gem and the Langrishe, that are remembered best in Deadwood.

Opened in the spectacular 'seventies, the Gem Theater played down every other amusement house that tuned its fiddles and lit its footlights in the gulch. It was the best known, the longest lived, and the last of the old mining-camp theaters. Its fame was blazoned from the Hills to Australia and South Africa, from San Francisco to Montmartre and back again to Shanghai. When it was burned in the beginning of the new century, not only did a weary, worn-out, old playhouse go up in flames, but a distinctive type of entertainment peculiar to the frontier passed out of existence. For half a century, since the first one was opened in San Francisco, the mining-camp theater had been a noisy center of recreation in every western gold camp of California, Colorado, Montana, Nevada, and the Hills. It filled a definite need in the lives of the hard-working, hard-living and hard-playing men of the new towns —men too vigorous and active, too filled with the excitement of making fortunes overnight, of breathing over-ozoned air, and of building a new country, to sit down quietly and take their pleasures vicari-

Footlights of the Frontier

ously. They must have a hand, a voice, or a foot in everything.

Mining-camp theaters were all alike and usually their lives were as brief as they were merry. When a gold camp grew into a quick young city or its gold veins pinched out and it was abandoned, the theater went on to the next new camp. Only the Gem lived to a decrepit old age. It had no other place to go. The gold rush to Deadwood Gulch was the last of its kind. Those that came after were closer to the railroads and before many years prospectors were going to gold stampedes in automobiles. So the mining-camp theater after a long life of prosperity and gayety died in Deadwood in the second year of a new century to which it did not belong.

The stage performances in these theaters varied with the house, the manager, and the demands of the patrons. Play and players at the Gem would have done credit to a theater dependent solely upon its drama. Many men and a few women well known later in better-behaved theaters contributed to its high dramatic standard blotted only here and there with rough variety acts. Charley Ross and Mabel Fenton did in the old Gem their vaudeville sketch that afterwards brought the twain high salaries in high-class houses, but their most noteworthy performance was a post-midnight act staged before the other players and a company of steady, late-staying patrons, when they were married by Justice Hall at four o'clock one morning. In '87 when the theatrical business was at its height the "Mikado" ran one hundred and thirty nights!

To the Gem Theater belongs the credit of discover-

Old Deadwood Days

ing the dramatic value of the Sioux Indian dances as a spectacle in a show instead of a terrifying prelude to bloody tragedy on the plains. The wars of the 'seventies scarcely were forgotten and the war whoops still were echoing through the mountains of the Great Spirit's hunting grounds, when the Gem recognized the theatrical worth of the real American folk dance. It was old Red Cloud, the Ogallala chieftain, who brought his band from Pine Ridge in the summer of 1880 for the performance that no one then realized marked an epoch in the world's folklore and entertainment.

Incidentally it was the gorgeous preluding parade of those Indians that first brought the Gem Theater into my line of vision. Robbie and I were sitting on the front steps exiled from our contemporaries and from our mother because Halle had diphtheria. We were not quarantined but we were encouraged to stay out of doors and away from other children. We walked all over the town and climbed the mountains but this afternoon we were tired. We had walked to the top of McGovern Hill in the morning, and we were a little bored too, when suddenly a burst of loud splendid music heralded something worth while. Whatever it was it would have to pass the narrow gap of Wall street.

"Look, Robbie," I exclaimed, "watch down there." In a moment our watching was rewarded. Along came the noisy band and behind it an array of war-bonneted Indians on horseback the like of which was of novel splendor even to us little Westerners. Their brilliant eagle feathers dipped and swayed as they rode. They were armed with bows and arrows and they let out blood-curdling whoops.

"Come," I said, jumping up and catching Robbie's hand in mine. "If we hurry we can see them again at Gold street." He was only two years old but his little steps never faltered beside mine. We stopped and saw them at Gold street, from the head of the Lee street stairs, and finally we raced down Shine street to the corner of Main where we had a full glorious view of them as they passed us and went on up to Pine street. We waited there until they came back and then made our interrupted rush home seeing the scraps of the gorgeous parade at every narrow opening along the way.

We were sitting on the steps again still talking excitedly when the General came home to dinner and asked us if we had seen the Indian parade. We both talked at once telling him what we had seen and asking what it meant. Old Chief Red Cloud and his band of warriors and squaws, he told us, were going to give an entertainment of Indian dances that night at the Gem Theater and they had been parading as an advertisement. Besides the old chief, himself, and his wife, there were Lone Wolf, Stands First, Slow Bear, No Water, Young Mule, Wamba-Gee-Sapa, Johnny-Come-Lately, Black Bear, Moccasin, Joker, Cha-Sha-Sha, and Opaga, and with them three Indian policemen—Fast Horse, Iron Crow, and Bear Run. We were enchanted with the names and Robbie furnished much glee for the three of us by trying to pronounce them all after the General.

They were going to dance war-dances and squaw-dances, and scalp-dances down at the Gem Theater

Old Deadwood Days

that night just as they did when they scalped people not so long ago. There would be choruses howled by the entire troupe and they would beat their tom-toms and all the excitement and splendor of Indian days would come back without the danger.

The ugly square front of the Gem Theater that we could see through a hole in the street where the house had not been rebuilt since the fire, took on an entirely new aspect. It enclosed a palace of adventure.

"If it wasn't for the diphtheria," I ventured, "we could go and see them, you and Robbie and I."

"Go and see 'em," Robbie said, his big dark eyes dancing.

The General smiled at us and shook his head. "No. Nice people like us don't go to the Gem Theater."

"Why?" I asked and he didn't give me any entirely satisfactory answer. It seemed a great waste of material to present such a magnificent spectacle in a place where nice people like us couldn't go.

With all its stage attractions, the compelling lure of the Gem still was the same as in all the other mining-camp theaters—the easy-go-lucky dancing for which the loose wooden chairs were cleared away at the end of the show; the bar in the corner by the entrance; and the curve of curtained boxes around the sides where pretty girls when they had finished their singing and dancing acts on the stage, beguiled the theater patrons to drink with them. It was a part of every girl's job—this "working" or "rustling" the boxes. They were the theater's best source of income. It was their importance that gave Johnny Burns, the manager, his title of "box-

Footlights of the Frontier

herder." A little air of mystery lurked in the dim lights behind those close-drawn, heavy curtains.

A man might watch the show, dance, take a drink with one of the girls, and go away and forget the Gem. But if he found his way up into one of the curtained boxes, he came again—and again. The dancing was gay and noisy, the music rhythmic and seductive, and at the end of every dance the caller sang out: "All promenade to the bar, and make room for the ladies." The last dance instead of being a waltz-timed "Home, Sweet Home," as it was up town and on Forest Hill, was a "Hack-Driver's Quadrille."

In the rooms over the theater the performers lived their irregular lives and sometimes, with the sharp report of a gun that carried far out beyond the Gem walls, they called attention to their tragedies and their loves.

Once a girl in her 'teens came out to sing at the Gem, believing blithely that she was starting on one of the lower rungs of a ladder that would lead her to theatrical fame and fortune. They said she drank champagne in one of the boxes that first night with a gay crowd. She probably never had tasted it before. In the middle of the night the party all drove to Sturgis. None of them believed she could be as naïve and innocent as she seemed. Back in her room above the Gem, sobered by a short hour's sleep, she shot herself at dawn.

She was only a few years older than I—a girl who should have been in high school, walking with her arm around her best girl friend at recess, and going to church with her family on Sunday. I couldn't

111

Old Deadwood Days

forget her. Father looked very grave when he talked about her at the breakfast table and the General said harsh things of Al Swearengen, the proprietor of the Gem. Mamma said nothing but I noticed she ate scarcely any breakfast. The *Pioneer* and the *Times* both ran long but very gentle stories. No one had a word of censure for the little suicide. Scores of girls came after her who knew nothing of the sinister meaning of the curtained boxes.

Frequently they drifted along for a while and then went the way of the little gun and the quick poison, but most of them slipped into the easy dusky way and forgot their clean young ambitions. Only one kicked up her little French heels and walked out into the daylight of Main street.

Long years afterwards when the Gem Theater was a memory and most of the ladies of the badlands had slipped out in a trailing scent of musk, a county official going over the ancient records of Smith, the undertaker, was appalled by the number of girls of the Gem and houses of like repute who had committed suicide in those hard, early 'eighties. He said no one ever had known how many there were. Many a case that had been pneumonia or mountain fever in the papers was laudanum or a bullet in the undertaker's record. Now and then a murder that could not be hushed, focused the town's attention, and inconsequent shootings were of common occurrence. No one paid much attention. It was an accepted phase of mining-camp life.

Futile shots flew about like angry words. Once Lou Desmond shot a girl who had stolen her lover from her, but the bullet glanced off the heavy steel

Footlights of the Frontier

of the lady love-pirate's corset and saved her life for further buccaneering. Once Flora Fleming shot at a discarded lover who had broken down the closed door of her room that erstwhile had stood hospitably open to him. Although her shot went wild, she was fined one dollar and costs in the police court.

Sometimes they didn't use guns. There was one singer at the Gem who, disregarding the code of her calling to trim up her topical song, used the name of a cautious admirer. He was sitting in a box and his anger at her audacity rose to such a pitch that he got up and threw all the chairs in the box at her. Evidently he was not experienced in the throwing of chairs because he didn't hit her. The orchestra ducked out of the way and the people sitting below him in the line of his poor aim made a hurried exit. Here was sensation of a sort that Al Swearengen did not care about. The reckless singer lost her job. The theater lost a patron. I don't know whether the man lost his reputation or not. Probably not. No one ever seemed to know exactly who he was.

A murder and suicide at the Gem Theater impressed me particularly because of the supreme disgust it aroused in Father. "Loved her so," he quoted with more scorn on the verb than most people heap on a horse thief. "Loved her so! It's a fine way to love a woman."

The crime, that had headlined itself into the morning papers, concerned him because he knew the young man's father. "A good, hard-working man," Father said he was.

"He doesn't seem to have brought up his boy very well," Mother ventured, and Father left the break-

Old Deadwood Days

fast table with a grumble about people not always being responsible for the kind of children they had. We all resented that and the day started unpleasantly all because of that Charley Wilson who had killed a woman and then tried to kill himself. I got the paper as soon as I could and went out and sat on the woodshed roof where I was tolerably safe from sudden interruption and read about it in detail. The girl, Kitty Clide, was a beer slinger at the Gem and Charley Wilson played in the orchestra. He had come to the Hills with his father in '76. He shot her in one of the blind-drawn upper rooms of the Gem early in the morning and killed her instantly. Then he turned his gun on himself but at first the doctors thought he was not fatally hurt. All he could talk about was that he "loved her so." Not even the badlanders sympathized with his manner of expressing affection. His father took him home and he died after two weeks of reiterating that he "did it because he loved her so."

The girl who refused the alternative of rustling boxes or shooting herself was Inez Sexton, a singer. Her voice, she said, was for sale; she herself was not. Working the boxes was beneath not only her standard of morals but her dignity as an artist. Being a clever and experienced woman and popular with her audience, she was able to cope with the situation for several months, but she was on bad terms with Swearengen who held back her salary and thought of various other schemes that might bring the proud artist to terms. None of them did. One mild night in May she lifted her little pointed chin and with a few well-chosen words to the manager anent misrepresentations, morals, and manners, walked out into the dimly lamp-lit street and up to the Wentworth house. She had neither money, friends, nor acquaintances, but Col. Cornell gave her unquestioning credit and spread the story.

Deadwood was a wide-open, careless, happy-go-lucky town. The Gem Theater, the dance halls, saloons, and gambling houses were its very life. But to throw a woman unwillingly into the ways of the badlands was entirely outside Deadwood's code. The benefit that was arranged for Miss Sexton by the church people from all the churches was one of the gala events of the town's history. Everybody who could play or sing gave his services. Professor Hirschfeld who spent a number of years trying to teach young Deadwood to play the piano as well as he did, was interested to the point of playing a solo. It was the *Waltz Caprice* from "Faust," which I remember distinctly because I was so enchanted with it that later on I persuaded him to teach it to me and I toiled long faithful hours trying to play it with his artistic finish. Miss Sexton, in a pale blue velvet gown trailing behind her, sang "It Was a Dream," and I remember that because Charity Martin sang it once at one of her own concerts in the later years when she had come to be the "Black Hills Nightingale," and I played it for her. We were too young to help with Miss Sexton's benefit but we gave considerable musical account of ourselves later, especially Charity. I don't remember the rest of the program because neither of us picked up any of the other numbers, but the concert was a great success. The hall was full and they made a lot of money for

Old Deadwood Days

Miss Sexton who bowed herself out of the gulch smiling and flinging roses, as it were, and everybody was as pleased as a prospector who has just struck it rich.

That was the only time the good people of the town ever gave a benefit for a lady of the Gem, but the Gem players themselves always were giving them for each other. Their masked balls were famous for the ingenuity of the costumes. Just by accident I saw one of the most bizarre of them all, the "cattle-brand dress." I would have tried it on but my mother wouldn't let me. Mother and I had gone down to Seebick's to see about a dress she was having made and he showed us the costume. It had been made in Chicago and he was finishing some slight alterations. The gown was of heavy black satin with a wide skirt that swept the floor all around and was finished with a lavish double ruffle. The little basque was tightly fitted, very low in the neck, and had short puffed sleeves. But the distinctive thing about it was the rich embroidery of cattle brands interspersed with roses, that covered the entire gown—wide skirt, little basque, short sleeves, and everything. It was very heavy embroidery and gorgeous with all the shades of red, blue, green, and purple. Not a cowboy who rode riotously into Deadwood and found his way to the Gem, nor a cattleman looking for a little diversion when he came to town, but could find the brand of his own cows on that gown. Mr. Seebick said it cost, with the perky little hat that went with it, more than four hundred dollars.

My closest glimpse of the Gem came one soft sum-

Footlights of the Frontier

mer night when Mr. Remer and I sat on our front steps and talked about people and life. The air was fragrant with the lilacs that bloomed beside the porch and filled with a mellowed mess of music from the dance halls, saloons, and the Gem Theater. The music brought our desultory conversation to the Gem.

"You would be surprised," Mr. Remer said using the word lightly and casually with no remote thought of the amazing revolution he was about to raise in my mind, "how nice some of those Gem Theater girls are—how much like other girls."

The night was bright only with stars and he was looking down toward the gray front of the theater so he didn't see my face. He had no way of knowing that my known world had dashed into space like the craziest comet leaving me with no familiar code for a foothold. Nice men *did* go to the Gem Theater. Its dull walls *did not* enclose a continual orgy of violent scarlet sin. A lifetime of standards called for instant and complete readjustment. All my life the windows of the drab Gem front had looked up at me as the eyes of hell. Everything and everybody I knew were safely on the outside. The interior was peopled with lost souls. And now I was told this was not true.

He went on talking in a nonchalantly interested way about these Gem Theater girls but I remember nothing else he said. The thing he had told me was that he—a man of my own world, my friend, a man with whom I danced and dined and walked and drove—he knew these girls of the lost lands, the badlands. He knew them personally and talked with

117

them as he was talking with me now. And they were not so different! His rich low voice went on easily and he didn't seem to be conscious at all that the high protecting walls of the social order in which I had grown up, were crashing around our heads.

In a tent saloon on Main street a man with a beautiful baritone voice was singing:

"I would not chide thee, chide thee, Marguerite,
Nor mar one joy of thine so sweet."

From beyond the open doors of the theater came the brassy strains of the "Mikado."

"The flowers that bloom in the spring, tra la," the music lilted, "have nothing to do with the case."

They were all mixed up, too. The sharp black-and-white of life was all smeared into a purple-and-gray smudge.

But in the end the Gem Theater worked out its destiny according to the hard and fast rules of melo-drama. The cards were stacked against it at the last. Shabby and unalluring, it met the rivalry of a street-long carnival in its last days. In every saloon a vaudeville show was given. String orchestras sobbed and rippled. Girls with throaty voices sang popular ballads. Banjos and guitars twanged. In the street outside the Salvation Army and a little band of Mormon missionaries a block or two apart, lifted up their pleading voices. And down in front of the Gem Theater a few paltry pieces of brass struggled futilely to recall the straying allegiance of the old theater.

Al Swearengen, dark and low-browed, who man-

Footlights of the Frontier

aged the Gem Theater all its life, suggested in face
and character the old-time villain of melodrama,
and he came to the last act of the play true to the old
technic. People said he abused the girls at the
theater. He quarreled so violently and disastrously
with his wife that she customarily wore at least one
black eye and frequently limped. Finally he
divorced her for infidelity. Once he was fined ten
dollars and costs in Judge Hall's court for beating
up "Swede Lena" when she was a spectator in his
theater. He said she "didn't conform to the rules
of the house," which might have meant anything.
Yet his years of prosperity were long and full. He
was said to have handled more money than any other
man in Deadwood. An ordinary night's business
was five thousand dollars. It was known to run as
high as ten thousand. After the burning of the Gem
Theater Swearengen left Deadwood, broke, his
greedy cruel hands empty of the thousands upon
thousands of dollars in gold that had passed through
them. A few years later he was killed by a locomotive in the railroad yards at Denver where he was
trying to steal a ride—a common tramp. From all
his long years of glittering success he had salvaged
nothing—money, happiness, nor friends.

Jack Langrishe and his wife turning their faces
away from Broadway and the Strand, lifted up their
eyes unto the hills. The lure of the West was in
their blood; the love of the mountains in their
hearts. They could have played in any place they
chose. And they chose the frontier. From the time
they opened in San Francisco in the early 'fifties,
they were known wherever men dug gold as the

Old Deadwood Days

"mining-camp players." Simultaneously with every gold discovery, it was said, Jack Langrishe appeared with a theater under his arm—a real theater with no dance-hall or bar attached, a house of clean, clever comedy, melodrama, and tragedy, to which men took their families, and whose doors never opened on Sunday. He built more theaters on the frontier than any other man who ever lived.

Early in '76 he came to Deadwood and for a short time leased the Bella Union variety theater giving it, during his tenancy, a strange new character that must have astonished its logs walls. During his short lease Wild Bill was killed by Jack McCall in the Number Ten saloon next door, and Langrishe gave the use of the theater for the rump court that tried and acquitted McCall. As everybody knows, McCall's acquittal did him little good because the court was without authority or recognition and when the Federal authorities heard about it, he was brought to trial again, convicted, and hanged.

The Bella Union's neighbor on the other side was more peaceable. It was a narrow wedge of a lunch counter calling itself humbly, "Crumbs of Comfort Along the Crack in the Wall."

In the late summer of '76, Langrishe built a theater of his own on Main street opposite the alley and stairs that were Gold street. It was a crude structure of logs and lumber with a canvas top that proved to be of no value at all as a roof. On the night of the opening the rain fell in torrents on "The Banker's Daughter," and the crowd that had come out to see her. Audience and performers alike were drenched, but no one went home and no one was dis-

120

Footlights of the Frontier

couraged. A more dependable covering was put on before it rained again.

This theater, Langrishe lent to the Episcopalians for their first service in Deadwood. Mrs. Dennee who had worked hard to make the service possible, played the hymns and she and her young daughter, Lizzie, not counting her little girl, Maude, were the only ladies present. There were one hundred men. Nothing like that ever happened again in the gulch. A lay reader read the service.

Just in time to be burned down in the big fire, Langrishe built a second and better theater that enjoyed a brief glorious existence. As he and Jimmy Martin, a member of his company, stood looking at the ruins the next day, he remarked: "Well, Jimmy, I guess we'll have to put out the 'standing room only' sign. There is not a slab left to sit on."

It had been a proud theater with boxes in which Deadwood ladies in evening gowns gave smart theater parties—parties that did not impress the rest of the audience at all according to a story Mr. Bonham told me once. He said that was the only time he ever remembered "seeing Jack Langrishe floored."

"Mrs. Adams, wife of the first postmaster, was a large fine looking woman," Mr. Bonham said, "very stylish and well dressed. She went to the Langrishe Theater a great deal and usually had a box party. Finally she and some of the other ladies got some opera glasses that they used with a good many airs. The theater was so small that they had no need of them but they looked stylish.

"One night an old prospector who had been at the theater a few nights before and noticed Mrs. Adams and her friends, came in and sat down in a front seat. He was carrying a board about two feet long by half a foot wide that he had fixed up with two holes. Into these he had stuck two beer bottles. When Langrishe came on, the prospector raised his board with an affected air and looked through his bottles at the stage. For a moment Jack Langrishe—artist and experienced actor that he was, forgot his lines. He never had looked through that end of a beer bottle before. The whole performance halted for a moment until the company could control its merriment. The comedy was all out in front. Mrs. Adams, looking down through her mother-of-pearl glasses, was as much amused as anybody.

My only personal acquaintance with the Langrishe company was through the members who stayed in Deadwood after the Langrishes were gone. Fanny Price had married Judge Gaffey and Jimmy Martin had gone to work on a local paper. Mrs. Gaffey was the first real actress I ever knew and while the acquaintance was very casual, it englamoured life considerably for me. I used to go out of my way to speak to her and see her smile. Once the General took me to see her play in Esmeralda at Nye's Opera House and I had to pinch myself to remember that she was the same woman who went about in the social life of the town like other women and sometimes spoke to me.

I knew Jimmy Martin slightly and pleasantly too, but the marvel and the wonder of the Langrishe stock company so far as it touched my interest was my friend Maude Dennee. She was a little girl like me. We were in the same Sunday-school class. She

Footlights of the Frontier

had a father and a mother who were particular about what she did and where she went, just as mine were. Her mother and mine called on each other. We seemed to be the same kind of little girls with the same sort of home life and background, yet she had played child parts with the Langrishe stock company. She was familiar with another life entirely. She knew that enchanted land they called "behind the scenes." She had played Little Eva and one of the small children that the lady in East Lynn deserted and then came back and wept over through the window; and the sad-eyed little girl who wanted her father to "come home with her now," and I don't know how many more. I couldn't find out as much as I wanted to from her because she seemed to think there was nothing special to tell. Nothing to tell! Go round to the back door of the moon and turn on the starlight and have nothing to tell! But the experience set her a little apart—made of her a personage a little different from the rest of us. She told me once that Miss Price who had played child parts with Booth told her that many actresses had begun that way. It was a good way to begin, she said. I asked her, a little awed, why she gave up her career when she was so well started, and she said her mother wouldn't let her go away with the Langrishes and there was no one left to play with in Deadwood.

"Didn't you love it?" I asked. "Didn't you love it awfully?"

"Oh, yes, of course. Of course I did. It was perfectly lovely. P-e-r-fectly lovely, if I hadn't been so scared. Miss Chambers—you know she was

Old Deadwood Days

the leading lady—said that was stage fright and that nobody had it always. But I did. Every time I played. I was always forgetting my lines because I was so scared, and my knees always shook. I was just as scared as we were that day General Dawson took us down to see the Indians. You remember that, don't you?"

I certainly did remember that. The General had taken us down to the Mammoth Corral in Fountain City to see Red Cloud and his band of Indians. There were millions of Indians there and they had their faces all daubed up with red and yellow paint, and they all wore war bonnets, Red Cloud's eagle feathers trailing on the ground. The General introduced us to him and to some of the lesser chiefs whose war bonnets didn't trail, and we shook hands with them, each of us holding tight to the General with our other hand. Then an old Indian took one of Maude's long brown braids in his hand, laughed, and said something in his own tongue to the General. She was as good as scalped. Didn't the General know it? I wondered in a panic. Why didn't he do something instead of just holding her by the hand and talking along to the Indian? I wished he had his army sword that hung on the wall in his room. I closed my eyes to shut out the bloody sight, and even in the midst of my very real grief for the disaster that had befallen Maude, I felt a selfish satisfaction in the security of my own little shingled head.

The next I knew we were all three walking back up Main street, obviously unharmed and safe. The General holding us each by the hand, talked pleas-

124

antly about the Indians and seemed entirely unconscious of any narrowly escaped danger. But for Maude and me it was a long time before tranquillity was restored.

If that was the way it felt to look out across the footlights, I didn't blame her for giving up her career.

Jimmy Martin told me about the Langrishes one night behind the scenes at Nye's Opera House where he was kindly helping us with a Sunday-school entertainment. He had beckoned to me when I finished reciting the "Burial of Moses," to come and sit beside him on a scenery doorstep. He said it was too bad I never had seen the Langrishes and he appealed to Maude, sitting on the other side of him, for her enthusiastic corroboration.

Mrs. Langrishe, he said, was one of the greatest dramatic geniuses this or any other country ever produced. But she always would be unappreciated and unknown to fame because she would live and die on the frontier.

"She loved the stars above the mountains," he said, "better than any on the boards, and western sunshine more than bright white lights. She was one of the greatest of character actresses and far ahead of her day and generation."

He was talking to Maude and me as though we were grown up critics and we were so flattered and absorbed that Maude forgot she had to go on and sing until Irene, having finished "Douglas, Douglas, Tender and True," hunted her up and told her they were waiting.

When the change in half his listeners had been

Old Deadwood Days

effected, Mr. Martin continued. "Those who saw Mrs. Langrishe in the Black Hills," he said, "did not know her in her prime. They saw a lady well advanced in years who even in her youth had never been beautiful. Her voice, once round, full, and musical, was worn out through illness and excessive use, and often was beyond her control. When you remember that for years she not only played the heaviest of heavy parts in five-act tragedies or melodramas nightly but also wound up the performance with a farce, the wonder is that she had any voice at all left. With all this she still was a great actress."

The last strains of "In the Gloaming" floated back to us with a melancholy that the happy applause scattered just as it had after Douglas and Moses. Maude came back and sat down with us again and the doorstep that had been creaking under the three of us, gave way under the fourth and we had to move to a garden bench that was more dependable. The change shifted Mr. Martin's reminiscences from Mrs. Langrishe to her husband.

"Jack Langrishe was born in Dublin, reared in the United States, and lived his artistic life in the West," he biographed. "He was a great actor and abundantly able to shine in the very best organizations but he preferred his own company, his own theater, freedom of thought, freedom of action, and the mountains of the West. He wanted always to be able to do as he pleased, spoil a matinée if he wanted to. He hated matinées.

"Do you remember," he asked Maude, "when you had just died as Little Eva one afternoon, and the

126

slow music was still playing, and he turned on all the storm and hail in the thunder box and rang the curtain down with a big old-fashioned dinner bell? He kept ringing that bell like a man at a railroad eating house."

Certainly Maude remembered and while they both laughed she shuddered a little. "I most did die that day," she said. "I most died of fright. I didn't know what was happening. It's a wonder I stayed dead till the curtain was down. And I was awful glad to see my mother in the wings when I came off."

Jimmy Martin laughed. "Langrishe said he wanted to give Little Eva a good send-off, and he asked Mrs. Langrishe if she didn't think the effects helped the scene. It was a poor house anyway. We never got good matinée houses."

Farther removed from the Langrishe than the broken lengths of street that stretched between them at the time the great fire swept them both out of the gulch, was the Bella Union, Deadwood's first theater. From its opening early in the summer of '76, it kept, except for the short lease to Langrishe, its disreputable character and its fairly good variety bills.

The only effort at entertainment preceding the Bella Union, was in the Melodeon on the corner of Main and Wall streets where, on a makeshift stage at the end of the long gambling room, Lobster Jack sang songs and Dick Brown played the banjo. Once they had a minstrel show.

The Bella Union, a typical mining-camp theater with variety acts, dance hall, gambling games, and

Old Deadwood Days

seventeen curtained boxes facing the stage, was housed in a log building with a sawdust-covered dirt floor. But it had the first piano that ever came into Deadwood—an old-fashioned square instrument that had traveled two months by bull train from the river. The opening was advertised by a gorgeous parade in the morning with flag-decorated wagons drawn by beautiful blooded horses, and at night the house was packed to the doors. In the beginning all was merry and auspicious. Yet the Bella Union, in its three and a half years of life, was the scene of more unbilled gory melodrama than any other half dozen places in turbulent old Deadwood. Everybody with an ugly blood-and-thunder tragedy in his heart brought it in and spilled it over the sawdust of the Bella Union.

At its door Bummer Dan was killed because the bartender saw only his gaudy borrowed coat and mistook him for Slippery Sam. At the steps leading up to its stage, Shaunessy of Cheyenne was killed by Dick Brown who shot him after Shaunessy's wild-flung ax had just missed his lady love singing sentimental ballads to the banjo accompaniment of the beguiling Brown to whom she had transferred her affections. Eugene Holman of the minstrel show had been almost decapitated by the ax.

Once the pioneer piano was hushed while a marriage service, Lohengrined by bullet shots, was read beside its rosewood carving. A man and woman, billed for a musical act, had come in a few weeks before. There was nothing unusual about either of them, personally or professionally. The man was dark and foreign looking and played the piano with

Footlights of the Frontier

only average skill. The woman was pretty but tired and unhappy looking without much sparkle in her light voice. Even though they obviously were bored and weary with each other, they made no friends. Theirs was one of the most negligible acts on the bill yet it created the great sensation.

One night just before they came on, a quiet gray-looking man walked in and found a seat on the aisle in the middle of the house. He was a stranger but Deadwood in '76 was full of strangers and he attracted no attention until the close of the act. While they bowed to perfunctory applause he made his way, still unnoticed, toward the stage and fired twice at the musical team. Both shots went wild and before he could fire again the piano player had pulled a gun and shot the stranger. The woman, sobbing and hysterical, was on her knees beside him before the crowd had gathered. He put out his hand to hold her and spoke to one of the men beside him. "Bring him here, too," he said. "Don't let him get away."

A doctor who had been in the audience rose and shook his head at Billy Nuttall, the manager of the house. "He's done for."

The piano player who had made no move, came over and stood facing the woman across the man he had shot. He held his smoking gun until some one took it out of his hand.

The wounded man beckoned to two or three men around him. "I want to ask a favor of you fellows," he said with a little difficulty. "I'm going to die. That's all right. I tried to kill him and he got me instead. I can't live but a few minutes. This woman is my wife. She ran away with this man nearly two years ago and I've been hunting for them ever since. I want some of you to go out and find a priest and as soon as I am dead I want you to see that this man marries this woman. Not to-morrow nor some other day. Just as soon as I am dead. I want them married here beside my dead body. Before you move me. Promise me."

A dozen men promised. Two started at once on the quest. When they came back with the priest the man was dead. The piano player, urged by Jimmy-Behind-the-Deuce, went around and stood beside the woman who was crying quietly. The priest stood on the other side of the dead man.

"Do you take this woman?" he began while audience, performers, gamblers, and bartenders gathered around hushed and awed. Every sound in the noisy place was stilled. You could have heard a poker chip fall into the sawdust.

"According to the rite of our Holy Mother, the Church—" The priest's grave, young voice brought something holy into the sin-smoked air. A tense, uncanny silence followed his "Amen," as though the crowd were waiting for the peal of an organ and a breath of incense. It was broken only when Donan of the *Pioneer* who had been standing with bowed head in the back of the house, pushed forward toward the stage. The orchestra's piano player struck the first chord of the Mendelssohn Wedding March before he remembered suddenly the man, almost at his feet, who had arranged the marriage.

The second wedding at the Bella Union was a lighter, gayer, more conventional affair, more to the

Footlights of the Frontier

liking of Billy Nuttall. It was scarcely a month later that Fannie Bean and Charley Gilday were married before a large audience that had been watching their act. The full theater orchestra played the wedding music gayly. The first violin remembered from some misty past, "The Voice that Breathed o'er Eden," and whispered it through the ceremony that Judge Hall, listening, stretched to more impressive length. At the close of the ceremony the orchestra leader introduced Mr. and Mrs. Gilday to the audience, enumerating all their fine qualities and extolling their high abilities, after which in the name of the company he presented the bride with a gold watch and chain, and the audience applauded loudly just as though it had been part of a play.

The McDaniels Theater was built on a placer claim which turned out to be much more precarious than just plain sand. It didn't have to wait for the rains to descend and the floods to come. The miner descended with pick and shovel and pan to work his claim and quick was the fall of that theater. The only thing I ever heard about the McDaniels was the story Paul Rewman told me about the rousing welcome to General Crook that was given there the night the building was finished. Mr. Rewman recalled the event distinctly because he had been working on the roof and he drove the last nail in the last shingle after General Crook arrived in camp. He took his pay for work in tickets to the meeting instead of in gold dust, the current coin of the camp. General Crook held an informal perambulating reception up and down Main street

131

when he arrived. He shook hands with everybody along the way and remembered everybody he ever had seen before, even those he had escorted out of the Hills the year before, chief among them Captain Tom Russell, big and impressive looking, who was one of the Gordon stockade party that went through the hard winter of '74 and '75 only to be ordered out pleasantly but firmly by United States troops in the spring.

So far as sensational entertainment was concerned we needed the theater less than most communities because so much raw real drama trod the Gulch, occasionally leaping onto the mountain side, at least as far as the first terrace. Several shootings dashed at our front steps. When a band came booming up the street, it always was wise to wait and see what followed. Deadwood's everyday life was melodrama.

Once I was waiting on the corner of Main and Shine streets for Father whom I could see coming across the Red Creek bridge, when I heard a particularly glad exultant burst of brass from down the Gulch, and looking in its direction I saw an excited crowd of people coming along shouting and cheering. They progressed slowly and were not yet near enough for me to find out what it was about when Father came across the street looking very cross. He threw one disgusted glance down toward the noisy crowd but he didn't stop.

"Come on," he said to me shortly with a little jerk of his head that showed angry annoyance.

"What is it?" I asked hippety-hopping along up the steep sidewalk in an effort to keep up with his long stride. "What's the band playing for? Why can't we wait and see it?"

"We won't help to swell any such lawless hoodlum crowd. Come along."

Bill Linn lounged his six feet seven out of the low door of Kelly's grocery store on the other side of the street just then and came over where we were. If it had not been for him I probably never would have heard the story of Bill Gay. But as he and Father talked it over indignantly, I got the whole tale of a jubilant welcome to a cold-blooded murderer.

Bill Gay had been a miner and a prominent citizen of Deadwood Gulch in the early days and the town of Gayville had been named for him. He had a pretty young wife of whom he was desperately jealous—with good cause it seemed—but he had not the excuse of jealousy when he shot young Forbes, an inoffensive, not overbright boy in his late 'teens. Bill had caught him carrying a note from Mrs. Gay to one of her admirers. His wrath ramped high above his reason and he shot and killed the boy. Father had sentenced him to a long term in the penitentiary and now, less than three years later he was coming back, pardoned by the governor of the territory and receiving this exuberant musical welcome. Sheriff Manning who had taken him to the penitentiary when he was convicted was foremost in the home-coming welcome. He had met the stage somewhere in Elizabethtown, transferred Gay to his own buggy, and they drove uptown behind the high-stepping horses that danced to the music of the band.

Bill Linn walked along with us and we turned

Old Deadwood Days

on Williams street before the procession came into view. Several times after that I heard about Bill Gay. He went out on a ranch. Later on he discovered a lignite coal bank on his land that seemed to be valuable. Then recklessly he went to Montana and when he got mad and killed a man up there, they hanged him.

For a man who did not believe in capital punishment, Father seemed unreasonably glad about that.

One night a near-murder raged down Williams street to our very doorstep where it seemed to develop for everybody except those most concerned, into a near-comedy. Agnes McGill always had seemed an inoffensive neutral sort of person until that night when she raced down the hill behind a fusillade of shots and a fleeing man. She stirred up a terrible rumpus and the General went out and took her gun away from her and demanded an explanation.

"What's the matter with you? You can't mess up a nice night like this? What's the trouble?"

The man whom the General had called Jack, sat down on our lowest step groaning and holding his shoulder. Blood was oozing out of his sleeve. The General, with Agnes' gun safe in his possession, took a look at Jack and sent Gaylord into the house to telephone for Dr. Wedelstaedt. He went very unwillingly.

"You're not much hurt," the General said gruffly. "Come on, I'll take the two of you home. What did you do it for, Agnes?"

Just then Wilber Smith, the young deputy sheriff, and I came along from the Cushmans where we had

Footlights of the Frontier

been sitting on the steps with Irene and Norman Mason, and Wilber deserted me for this criminal case he found waiting at our terrace. As they all started up the hill, and Gaylord came back from the telephone with a rush, reinforced by Robbie, to join them, I heard the woman say:

"Oh, I love him so! I couldn't help it, I love him so!"

More Charley Wilson stuff, I thought to myself. Guns and great love seemed to go together in the lives of the badlanders.

Real life drama and adventure were so close and so insistent that we could not understand people taking pleasure in danger for danger's sake. We were excused from school one spring afternoon to see the amazing spectacle of a man walking a slack wire that had been stretched across Main street between the McLaughlin building and the Merchants Hotel. We went in a mob with wide eyes and open mouths. But why did he do it? He didn't have to. Life as we knew it with its commonplace necessities, offered danger enough. Indians, outlaw bronchos, deep mines, blasts of dynamite, people who loved too much and carried guns to prove it—why hunt danger?

With the opening of the new opera house, and the close approach of the railroad, regular traveling companies left the beaten theater trails and played Deadwood for a week or more, but never, after the Langrishe company, did anyone of them stay long enough to be a part of the life of Deadwood. They came and went as in any town, creating only a transient interest—even Grace Hawthorne, who opened

135

Old Deadwood Days

the opera house and played an extensive *repertoire* that included "Camille," and who stayed long enough to rent some furnished rooms and keep house. But we were too close now to the "end of the track" which changed so often in the late 'eighties that we never used a name—not Rapid City, nor Sturgis, nor Whitewood, just "the end of the track." These people had not staged it far enough really to "belong."

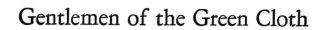

Gentlemen of the Green Cloth

Chapter 5

GENTLEMEN OF THE GREEN CLOTH

THEY were the lily-fingered leisure class of Deadwood — the gamblers who seemed never to toil nor spin, yet always were arrayed in fine linen and broadcloth fresh from the tailor's iron. They appeared on the streets in the early afternoons immaculately and expensively attired, quiet-mannered, and soft-spoken. They strolled up and down Main street with a magnificent leisure that was conspicuous even in Deadwood Gulch where all the people had time to attend to their important affairs without hurrying and scurrying and getting up in the morning before they were awake. All Deadwood sauntered easily, yet there was something about the leisureliness of the gamblers that was outstanding.

No one ever saw them in the morning. They slept until noon and lived their lives at night. Of course I never saw them at work—either the players or the dealers, but men who went about and gambled in casual, amateurish fashion said they always were the same. Always they wore their poker masks and spoke with quiet voices. Winnings and losses alike left them apparently unmoved.

"Gamblers never commit suicide unless it's a woman," Blondy McFarland of the *Pioneer* told me one day when I went into the office with a notice about a raspberry festival we were going to have for the church, and stayed to discuss an attempted suicide over on Siever street—a poor little alley of a street that one never heard of in any happy way.

"Three Sixes wasn't a professional gambler anyhow," Blondy explained. "He was a cook by trade and gambled for pleasure, but he never would have thought of suicide because he lost at faro. He took that laudanum because Swede Lena wouldn't marry him, and he was so set on dying that Dr. Babcock had to call in Marshal Garr to help him give the antidotes. Between 'em they succeeded in dragging Three Sixes back to his grief. Lena's reason for refusing to be Mrs. Three Sixes of Siever street was that her suitor smoked cigarettes.

"Then there was poor old Sam Curley back in the 'seventies," Blondy went on reminiscently. "He was a faro dealer but nothing could have happened in that game that would have made a quitter out of him. It was the little jig dancer did that."

I never before had heard Kitty LeRoy, the Gem Theater dancer, blamed for her own murder and her husband's suicide. That was one of Deadwood's historic tragedies and all the sympathy of the badlands and such as filtered down through the pines of Forest Hill and the crooked streets that led to Ingleside was for the woman who had been murdered in her room over the Lone Star saloon by her husband —this faro-dealing Curley—who had then turned the gun on himself with the desired result. She had not known he was in town when he came to her room and accused her of being untrue to him.

"Deadwood gamblers," Blondy went on, "are all

Gentlemen of the Green Cloth

good losers—always. No one of them ever rushes
out into the dawn and puts a bullet through his head
the way you hear about 'em doing at Monte Carlo
and places like that. In Deadwood Gulch you've got
to be a good loser. That's what life on the frontier
is—chance. The professional gambler just goes a
little farther with the game, that's all."

Some one came in then and interrupted us and I
started for home. At the corner of Lee street I met
Mike Russell going home, too, and he slowed down
his usual pace of a run and three steps at a time up
the Lee street stairs, to walk with me. He was a
slim, charming little Irishman with long brown
whiskers blowing in the wind, and was a close friend
and hunting comrade of Buffalo Bill. He was the
only man in Deadwood who during South Dakota's
amusing experiment in prohibition, stopped selling
hard liquor over his bar while all about him, up and
down Main street, new saloons blithely opened their
unlicensed doors. He never had been a lawbreaker,
he said, and he didn't intend to begin then. No
minors came into his well-ordered place; no women
hovered about. Calamity Jane was the only woman
who ever could get a drink in his place. He said
she was the exception that proved the rule.

I still was interested in Blondy's philosophy of
gamblers and I told Mr. Russell about it. He said
it was true. A professional gambler was always a
good loser.

"He can play his last dollar and watch the cards
come up without the flicker of an eyelash. If he
wins, all right. If he loses, he borrows another dollar from the house and tries again. A fellow can't

lose all the time, you know—not playing faro. It's the squarest game there is. There's less percentage to the house and a man who watches the cases is bound to win part of the time. Besides, if a gambler has a run of bad luck and is broke for a week, it doesn't matter. His credit's always good.

"I'd rather trust the gamblers than some of these merchants around town. There's one that gives his check for his losses after he's notified the bank that it isn't good unless it's countersigned by his partners and he's told them not to countersign his gambling checks. They probably wouldn't anyhow. I had that out with the bank just yesterday and I got my money but I'll never take that old fellow's check again. I can't be bothered. And he'll never have any credit in my place. I hope he stays away. No professional gambler ever would do a trick like that. He always plays the game according to the rules. He never loses his temper and he never takes a drink when he's playing—very rarely at any time. This old fellow gets mad when he loses. But commit suicide? Never; he might miss a dinner."

"It's a pity," Father commented when I brought up the subject at the dinner table, "that the amateurs don't follow the example of the professionals and keep their drinking and their playing separate. They'd save themselves a lot of trouble. There's Jack Gray, for example. He was in my office this afternoon trying to find some way to get rid of a saloon that he won at poker last night unbeknownst to himself. He already has a miner's boarding house up at Terraville that takes all of his time and

Gentlemen of the Green Cloth

his wife's too. He said their only salvation was that his wife neither drank nor gambled."

Father was a little amused at Jack's predicament and Jack himself had been able to see the humor in a man's going out for a harmless bit of recreation of the evening and coming home all saddled up with a saloon that he didn't want.

"It's what a man gets for drinking when he's gambling," Jack had admitted. "You can't do both. You've got to decide which you're going to do and stick to it."

He had been trying to get drunk and play poker at the same time, he said, and so had the other fellow. There were just two of them. The rest had dropped out. They put up all the money they had and everything else they could think of. Jack said he had just had sense enough left to remember "the old lady owned half the boarding house," and leave it out of the pot. But he kept putting up mining claims and the other fellow didn't have as many as he had so he put up his little old saloon at Gayville and Jack won that and they quit.

This morning his wife had shown him a deed to a saloon she had found in his pocket.

"I've always known you bought large interests in saloons," she said, "but I never supposed you'd buy one out entirely. Couldn't you get enough to drink any other way?"

He didn't dare tell her he'd won it playing poker so he came down town to see if he couldn't make some kind of a deal with the other fellow to take his saloon back. But he couldn't give it to him. The loser said he had been trying to get rid of the

place for a long time. Anyway he would not re-
pudiate a debt of honor and he could not afford to
buy the place back.

"Now Jack's going to quit both drinking and
gambling," Father concluded, "and run his saloon."

Mother looked at me in a detached sort of way
as if we were the only people at the table, and asked
if I had given her raspberry festival notice to the
Pioneer. That changed the subject for a few moments but the General brought it back for further
amplification of the advantages of faro over roulette, stud poker, or the Chinese game of fan-tan.
He seemed to know a good deal about gambling
games and gamblers and perhaps a good deal more
of interest than he told, but it wouldn't have been in
accord with the established precedent in our house
for the younger generation to ask the older *how* it
knew anything. Only Chinese servants had that
prerogative. It was the very next morning that
the General carelessly tried to be facetious with
Wong.

"Where did I see you last night, Wong?" he asked
as the Chinaman set down the General's red-and-
gold, dragon-decorated mustache-cup filled to the
brim with hot, strong coffee.

"Hmm," Wong grunted with no change of expression on his face, "where I see *you?*" He shuffled out, closing the kitchen door behind him, and
took the subject of the night's revels with him.
Father smiled out of the corner of his mouth at the
General but no one said anything.

I was interested to know that the General's
knowledge had been acquired at first-hand. He

Gentlemen of the Green Cloth

gambled very rarely, I learned afterwards, but apparently he learned a good deal at a time.

The thing I could not understand was why there was anything wrong about gambling and the first time I got Father alone I asked him.

"Gamblers don't do any harm," I said. "They're nice well-behaved people and it's their own money they win or lose. What's wrong about it?"

"They are not producers," Father explained. "They're living on money somebody else makes. Money doesn't just grow, you know; somebody has to earn it all. That is why mining is one of the cleanest, most honest, and worth-while occupations in the world. The gold a man digs out of the ground is a new addition to the world's wealth. He takes it away from nobody. It never belonged to anybody before. Gold mining is a great business. Neither weather nor wars interfere with it. There is no danger of overproduction and no fluctuating market value."

He had forgotten all about gamblers and I brought him back just far enough to ask in what way professional men were producers. I couldn't quite say "lawyers" but I was thinking about them. They didn't dig anything out of the ground and shovel it into the world's treasure chest.

"A professional man sells his knowledge. You know the story of Grier and the mechanic? Something went wrong with some of the machinery up in one of the Homestake mills and none of their own mechanics could get it fixed. They sent down here to Deadwood for a man who had a local reputation as a mechanical genius and he went up and straight-

145

ened out the trouble in half an hour. When he sent in his bill for fifty-five dollars it seemed so big that it was referred to the superintendent. Mr. Grier thought it was rather large for half an hour's work and he sent word to the Deadwood mechanic that he would like an itemized statement. He got it promptly. 'Five dollars for work done. Fifty dollars for knowing how to do it.' "

There was another thing I sought to learn as long as I had found Father in an unusual mood for imparting information. Why did everybody think so highly of this quality of being a good loser? I had heard about it all my life. I knew that to be a poor loser was almost as bad as being a horse thief. It was not followed by such quick and fatal retribution but it brought down almost as much scornful contumely on one's head. Was it because it was peculiarly a western virtue that Deadwood thought so highly of it?

Father thought possibly, but in itself it was a worth-while virtue? He said it was a combination of courage, philosophy, and self-control. "A man didn't need a great deal more than that," he added.

Moreover, gambling in Deadwood was distinctly a masculine indulgence. I know of only two nice women who ever even saw gambling in action in Deadwood's earlier days, and neither of them seemed to have observed as closely as they should considering their rare opportunities. There may have been others but I only know about these two.

One was Sue Neill, a tall, witty, red-haired spinster who remained county superintendent of schools no matter what party was in power until she

Gentlemen of the Green Cloth

finally tired of it and went back to Kentucky where she came from. She said she could be a Republican or a Democrat or a Populist. She didn't see any difference. You couldn't tell them apart by looking at them or even by talking with them. She walked abstractedly down Main street one evening with an important notice for the *Pioneer* about examinations for county-school teachers. She went through an open door and looked around for desks, green-shaded lamps, and industrious scribblers. Instead, she found herself in the midst of faro layouts, poker tables, and roulette wheels. She gave one startled sweeping glance around and then smiled pleasantly at the astonished but friendly looking white-aproned man who gazed at her in amazement, the napkin in his hand poised in startled surprise above the mahogany bar he had been polishing. Half a dozen little drinks were held in suspense halfway between the bar and half a dozen drooping mustaches.

"I assure you, gentlemen," Miss Neill said easily, "I did not intend to come in here. It was a mistake."

The bartender dropped his napkin and bowed low. "I'm sure of that, Madam," he said. "The *Pioneer* office is next door."

They bowed formally to each other again and everybody else bowed, and the lady withdrew.

The other woman appeared with angry intent in Bedrock Tom's place late one night. She did not saunter in by mistake. She knew where she was going and why, and she slid quickly and quietly into the midst of things. All activities ceased from sheer amazement just as they had for Miss Neill. She said nothing and no one else spoke or moved during her brief stay. Everybody knew whose wife she was. She was bareheaded and wore her big dark gingham apron. Evidently the idea of looking for her husband had struck her suddenly and she had acted at once. He was playing poker at a table with three other men—and losing as usual—when she came in. The jack pot in the middle of the table was a magnificent heap of gold pieces and bills.

In the hush, the woman did not even glance at her husband as she flung herself against the table and with one curve of her arm swept the entire winnings into her voluminous apron. In the deeper silence that followed, while not a card fluttered, not a foot moved on the floor, and the roulette wheel and the clink of glasses were stopped, she strode out with her booty, and they let her go as though she had won it in a square game. No one ever mentioned it later or questioned her right to it. But never again did any gambler in Deadwood Gulch play poker with *that* woman's husband.

I don't remember, now, the name of the gambler that I came to be friends with in a simple matter-of-course sort of way. All the family had gone out of town but Father and I, and we were eating dinner one night in a Chinese restaurant—not one of the city sort with inlaid teakwood and ivory and gorgeous hangings and mysterious food, but one of those that Chinamen ran in Deadwood in earlier days —plain little places with good plain American food and nice plain prices. The place was crowded and when this man came in the only vacant seat was at our table. He was turning to go out when Father called to him by name.

Gentlemen of the Green Cloth

"Come and sit down with us," he urged.

After some hesitation and more urging the man finally accepted with a charmingly diffident manner and Father introduced him. He was a pale man with deep blue eyes and he talked easily enough. Several times after that he ate dinner with us, always on Father's special invitation. Then the family came home and we didn't eat down town and I saw nothing more of him except as I occasionally passed him on the street and spoke to him.

One day in the winter Father came home and asked me if I remembered the man. Then he turned his conversation to Mother. He said this gambler had come up to his office to see him and ask what he called "an unusual sort of a favor." There was no one else, he said, whom he could ask. He had a sister arriving the next week, with her daughter, to visit him. He said they were nice women and they did not know what his business was. They would be horrified if they knew and his sister would be hurt. He could get a vacation from his job of dealing faro for as long as they stayed, and he could keep on telling them quite honestly what he had been telling them all the years, that he had mining interests. He could manage that all right, but the thing he would not be able to explain to them was that he had no friends or even acquaintances among the ladies of the camp. He wondered if it would be asking too much if Mother and I would go and call on them. They would be at the Gilmore Hotel.

"You understand, Judge," he had said at the end as he rose to go, "that I know you may not want to say anything about it to your wife and if you don't, we'll forget it. I'll understand perfectly."

Father never promised that Mother would do anything but he did promise vehemently that he would ask her and he thought she would be very glad to call on his sister.

So Mother and I did and found them to be just what the faro dealer had said they were. He came with them one evening to return the call and Father and the General talked to him about his mining claims and how they were developing. They both showed a convincing and interested knowledge and everything was as pleasant as the clean-up of a rich pocket. The sister and niece left town without hearing anything about faro banks and open gambling, and the pale, gentle-mannered faro dealer dropped out of our lives. I don't know what became of him when the blue laws closed the gambling games in Deadwood, and players and dealers were scattered to the winds.

Then there was California Jack. California Jack first attracted my attention through his wife and child. He was the only professional gambler I ever knew anything about who had a family, and he didn't keep his intact for long. The General and I were walking down Sherman street one Sunday afternoon when we met them.

"How do you do, Mrs. California Jack," the General said with a flourish of his soft black hat and then he smiled at the little boy. The woman didn't seem to find anything strange in the name by which he addressed her. She was a well-gowned, rather pretty woman, but it was her make-up that

Gentlemen of the Green Cloth

interested me. I never had seen anything like it. She was heavily powdered and used no rouge except on her mouth, and with her dark hair and black eyes, was most striking. Ladies I knew used powder slightly but never rouge. Other women used rouge profusely. That was one way you could distinguish them. Mrs. California Jack looked very "distinctive" but not very happy. Her little boy was not more than two or three years old and he "favored" her—black-eyed and pale. He wore a little white *piqué* dress and red fez. Once afterwards, I saw them in Shoudy's market buying steak. They were dressed just the same as when I saw them on the street and looked just as artificial and exotic. Mr. Shoudy wrapped up the steak in heavy brown paper and handed it to Mrs. Jack and she went out holding her little boy by the hand. Probably she would go home and broil her steak and cook potatoes and make a dessert and set the table just like the housewives of Forest Hill and Ingleside. But somehow it was hard to associate her with everyday domesticity. Apparently that was the way she felt about it because the next I heard about her she had eloped with another gambler leaving the child behind.

Years afterwards when California Jack was on trial in the United States court for fraudulent application for a pension, he was acquitted for two reasons. One was that the members of the Deadwood bar who had known him for years and believed he did not understand the enormity of his offense, had asked clemency for him. The other and more potent reason with the soft-hearted judge on the bench was the little ten-year-old boy, pale, dark-eyed, and serious who sat beside his father throughout the trial.

It was during the winter of my great musical ambition when I was wont to get up every morning at five o'clock to practice three hours before breakfast, that I received more light on the fascinating subject of gambling. Charity Martin, known from the Belle Fourche to the Cheyenne and from Rapid City to Sundance, as "the Black Hills nightingale," was going to give a concert in the Miner's Union Hall at Lead and I was to play her accompaniments and a solo. If the concert was an artistic success we were going to give another in Deadwood and then perhaps, we would go tripping around through the Hills on a tour. It behooved me, therefore, to practice. I was learning the accompaniments to Kalliwoda's "Farewell," and an aria from "Ernani," but I left them until my fingers got warmed up a little.

I had lighted the lamp, set it on the side of the big square piano, had found my book of *arpeggio* studies, and run my fingers once up and down the keys, when I heard some one on the porch. It was not yet daylight and I stopped to listen, not alarmed but curious. The front door opened and closed softly, then the door into the front parlor swung halfway, and the General came in. He put his finger on his lips and motioned for me to go on playing. He was pale and a little haggard but he hadn't been drinking. I covered his coming in with loud *arpeggios* and he came and sat down beside the piano and told me about it in whispers. He said he had been playing poker all night with Johnny Otis, the "Montana Man" who seemed to have no other name, and Swede Johnse.

Gentlemen of the Green Cloth

"Did you win?" I wanted to know, playing the left hand very loud because I couldn't play them both at once and talk or listen, and I wanted to find out about all this.

"A little." He dug down in his pocket and pulled out a considerable roll. He peeled off a ten-dollar bill and gave it to me. "I'm going to give the rest to your mother. There isn't much. Swede Johnse got most of it. Johnny was cleaned. He started out winning but it was too big a game for him. Some men can play little games but when it comes to a big game they can't stand it. I don't know why. It's just the way they're built. But Swede—first he called Johnny on a pair of fours—fours! And he won five hundred dollars."

I was so excited I stopped playing and he waited for me to go on. I rattled the music on the rack and started on Chopin's "Polonaise Militaire." It's nice and noisy and I was going to play it at Charity's concert.

"Then," the General went on, "Swede called again and won another five hundred dollars. This time on a pair of fives. He's a great gambler, Swede Johnse. He's got the perfect poker face. You always can tell when Johnny has a good hand. Mike Russell told me that and I noticed to-night and he's right. When Johnny has a good hand he looks at it and then swallows hard two or three times. Most gamblers have some little mannerisms that give their hands away when you know them very well. Mike and I were talking about that early in the evening. You can make money by being observing and not saying anything. But Swede Johnse

153

—you can't tell a thing. And he won a thousand dollars to-night on a pair of fours and a pair of fives."

I struck the opening chords of the "Polonaise" again and kept the loud pedal on until he had time to get upstairs to his room. Then I stopped long enough to tuck my ten dollars down in the top of my high shoe. I wondered how I was going to spend it without arousing Mother's curiosity, and I finally decided I'd keep it dark until she forgot about whatever it was the General gave her. The early bird caught a nice fat little worm that morning.

I was beginning to think gambling was all claret and cake. All you had to do was to let strong drink alone, play faro, and watch the cases, and you could sleep until noon, wear good clothes, and stay up as late as you liked. Of course I wasn't considering taking up gambling as a profession but certainly there was something to be said for it. Then, late one afternoon I went with Father up to Central. He had to go up on a quick errand and come right back, so he took me with him.

We climbed up over the wheel into the middle seat of Fred Doten's standard hack that we hailed on Main street and started for Central and Golden Gate, going along slowly and picking up passengers as we went. When the hack stopped in front of the Wentworth Hotel to wait for some one, a man they called Johnny got down and announced that he was going into the Senate to win his fare to Central.

"Oh, no," Fred objected. "We'll be ready to go in a minute and we can't wait for you. The fare's only fifty cents."

Gentlemen of the Green Cloth

Yes, Johnny knew all that but he could make it in a minute and before he could hear further objections he had disappeared behind the swinging half doors of the Senate saloon and gambling house that stood next door to the Wentworth. Because Fred and all his passengers had some understanding of the gambling urge, we waited.

Johnny's minute grew into five, into ten, and twenty. The passengers began to grumble. Those who lived in Gayville, Central, or Golden Gate said their wives would be waiting dinner and getting cross. Father was afraid his client would get tired and go back up to Ragged Top, and he didn't want to miss him.

"A gambler when he gets up against a faro bank," mumbled a man on the back seat, "is worse than a woman getting ready to go to a dance. They don't care a color how long anybody waits."

Fred looked at his watch and shut the case with a snap. "It's more than half an hour now," he said to Mr. Remer who was sitting beside him hoping to get to the Father DeSmet mine where he lived and was paymaster, some time before breakfast. "Bill," Fred appealed to him, "you go in and get Johnny. We can't wait any longer. You're big and you look as though you had authority. Bring him by the ear if you have to."

Remer vaulted down over the high wheel and went after Johnny. Neither of them said anything when they came back almost at once. They just got in and we went on our way. But I noticed how Johnny looked. I suppose everybody else did too. They couldn't help it. Mr. Remer told Father and

155

me afterwards that he found the man beside the faro table, pale and drawn, coppering bets and writing orders on future wages. In his effort to win the fifty-cent fare to Central, Johnny had lost in a little more than half an hour, seventeen hundred dollars.

In the fall of 1890, about a month before the railroad came into Deadwood and the Sioux met final defeat at the battle of Wounded Knee, something happened that was new in the annals of Deadwood gambling. Father said it was a travesty on the law which never should be invoked in such personal frivolous fashion. Romeo Dwyer didn't think it was frivolous. To him it was a serious and hateful matter. The General said it was like a comic opera or a South American revolution. He grieved greatly because he was shut up in the house with an attack of rheumatism and couldn't get down town to hear all the inside gossip and get all the side-lights. I had to go down every day to see his partner, H. B. Young, and bring back all the news fresh from the badlands and the courts. That's how I came to know so much about it. The only trouble was that so many exciting events came off at night.

We saw the beginning from our bay window. The General had just hobbled down stairs for the first time and was very unhappy and cross until this entertainment came along. He leaned forward on his cane and looked out.

"That was the sheriff," he said with more interest than he had shown in anything for several days. Sheriff Knight, being one of the sons of the Anakims who were numerous in the Hills was not hard to distinguish. With the sheriff was Ben Garr. "They

Gentlemen of the Green Cloth

just walked pompously across Wall street, the sheriff ahead," he told Mother and Halle and me who had come to see what it all was about, "and went into Dwyer and O'Dell's."

A crowd had gathered by that time and we couldn't see what happened but in the course of time the crowd followed the excitement uptown. We heard about it from Father when he came home, and an elaboration from Mr. Young when he came later in the evening to see the General.

The sheriff, followed by the city marshal had proceeded down Main street that afternoon to Dwyer and O'Dell's saloon and gambling house and, on complaint of the mayor, arrested the proprietors and all those running gambling games. The authorities had taken possession of all the paraphernalia of play which included faro tables, faro boxes, check boards and cases, roulette wheels and apparatus, and two tub games.

"What for?" thundered the General. "What's the matter with Romeo?" He didn't care a copper about Romeo but his rheumatism was making him miserable and he hated staying in the house, and nobody had told him yet why Dwyer and O'Dell had been arrested. Father, sitting over at his desk playing solitaire, suggested satirically that it might be because there was a state prohibition law that was supposed to have gone into effect a year before, and a state law against gambling about which no one seemed to know anything.

"Yes," Mr. Young said, "Star knows about it," and they all laughed. That seemed to be the crux of the whole thing.

157

Old Deadwood Days

Sol Star had just been reëlected mayor of Dead-wood and Romeo Dwyer had worked against him. A little rash, to say the least, because it was impossible to defeat Star, partly because of his flour mill on upper Main street. As long as that mill ground wheat, it was said, no one in Deadwood went without flour. Anyone in need could get a sack of flour any time without money and without price. Those who could, paid for it at their convenience. Those who could not, never heard anything about it. Sol Star never failed to give Deadwood her daily bread. Of course when he ran for mayor people remembered the hand that fed them. There seemed always to be enough of these to elect him.

Romeo Dwyer never had been in need of flour. All his life there had been cake baked and frosted at his hand. He was under no obligations to the perennial candidate for mayor and for some reason or other, wanted to see him defeated. He got out and worked hard against him and of course Star heard about it.

Being already in office when the election was over and the votes counted, Mr. Star discovered at once that Romeo Dwyer with his partner, Jack O'Dell, was breaking the law by operating a saloon and gambling house right in Sol Star's nice well-behaved bailiwick. He lost no time in having them arrested, assuming blandly that they were the only men in town engaged in any such lawless business.

Dwyer and O'Dell and five men who were running games in their place appeared that night in justice court where their cases were continued and they were released on their own recognizance. Mr.

Gentlemen of the Green Cloth

Young said their games would all be running again before midnight. They were. But the next day Romeo and O'Dell and a lone faro dealer were arrested again, taken into court again, and released again.

By now Romeo was getting mad. He had accepted the first arrest philosophically enough. He had expected to pay some price for his futile political activities, but the second arrest was unreasonable. He hadn't recovered all his gambling devices and he couldn't afford either the time or the money involved in going into court every day and opening up new games every night. Furthermore he couldn't keep men to run the games if they were to be arrested every day. Romeo's wrath rose high to action. If there were laws against gambling and against selling liquor, and Star wanted them enforced in Deadwood, all right. But Dwyer didn't propose to be the one solitary law-abiding member of his craft in Deadwood Gulch. He went before a justice of the peace and made complaint against everybody in town who ran a gambling house or was employed in one. Deadwood would have gone dark very suddenly if some one had not warned the saloon men. When the warrants were served nobody had any gambling tools or devices. No one ever had heard of such things. A roulette wheel? What did it look like? A faro bank? They might ask D. A. McPherson. He was cashier of the First National. He ought to know about banks. The sheriff and the city marshal were both angry and amused—mostly angry. They were sick and disgusted anyway with all this buffoonery—this making a mock of law enforcement.

159

Old Deadwood Days

I forgot to tell the General about Hattie Bell being arrested just then in the midst of everything for running a disorderly house. Mr. Young had mentioned it but I didn't see that it had any bearing on the gamblers' war. It seems it had. The General found it in an obscure corner of the paper the next morning at breakfast and remarked dryly that he thought "Star was in poor business dragging a man's mother into this embranglement."

"A man's mother!" I expostulated. What had mothers to do with these brawling battles of the badlands?

"Yes," the General was waxing indignant, "a man's mother. Just because she keeps the 'Castle' over in Fink's Flats is no reason for dragging her by her bleached locks into a political-gambling scrap that she doesn't know anything about.

"Hattie Bell," he advised us slowly and impressively, "is Romeo Dwyer's mother. Because Star is mad at Romeo he must needs have her haled into court. Is he laboring under the impression that she is the only woman in town following the oldest profession? Does he think Hattie and Romeo are all the brunette sheep he has in his nice white flock?"

Hattie pleaded guilty, paid a fine of fifteen dollars, and went back to her castle.

Somebody else was arrested and had his playthings taken away from him every day, but they all seemed to get them back and go on about their business except the luckless Romeo.

And to heap the measure of righteousness Tommy Ryan concluded it an opportune time to avenge

Gentlemen of the Green Cloth

some little private peeve he thought he cherished, and he swore out a warrant against Dwyer for carrying concealed weapons. They had a fight on the street about it but nobody paid any attention to that, and later Ryan went into Dwyer's place and assaulted him with a chair. Dwyer retorted with a beer glass thrown with such skill and speed that it cut Ryan's head open, and brought the expert thrower under arrest again, this time for assault with a dangerous weapon. A beer glass it appeared, was a more dangerous weapon than a chair.

Thereupon some "boys" took advantage of the general confusion to open a little snap game on Lee street one evening after dark. But a deputy sheriff swooped down on them, raked in their paraphernalia, and arrested everybody around including Patsy Carr and Tex Rankin who had a saloon on the corner. Carr and Rankin were entirely innocent. They knew about the law against gambling and they were not lawbreakers. They merely kept a saloon. They hadn't heard of the prohibition law. Nobody had but Mike Russell and there was no use in his passing on his knowledge. No one would have believed *him*. Carr and Rankin had just leased the rear rooms of their place of business to the owners of the game. How did they know what they were to be used for? So everybody went free again, the owners of the game having become lost in the shuffle.

On Thanksgiving Eve when the gambling contingent was looking forward to a day with little cause for thankfulness, the city authorities closed up Wardner and Gates' saloon on Lee street and

took possession because the owners had kept open
on Sunday. That was an awful thing for them to
do. It didn't occur to anyone that all days were
alike to the state prohibition law and men had just
as much right to sell liquor on Sunday as on Monday or Friday. On Thanksgiving Day a warrant
was issued again for all those connected with the
faro game at Carr and Rankin's. But when the
sheriff arrived there was no one in the place but a
solitary rounder toying idly with a stack of "coppers." The sheriff put the coppers in his pocket and
went home to his turkey and cranberry sauce. The
last wish-bone was picked and the last crumb of
pumpkin pie disappeared in the midst of what
seemed to be victory for the law. Not a gambling
game of any kind was running in Deadwood Gulch.
Never had that happened before since the first card
was turned and the first bet coppered in the winter
of '75 and '76. The gamblers stood around the
streets looking as sad as they could considering their
carefully cultivated poker faces. Certainly it was
a poor Thanksgiving Day for Deadwood's leisure
class.

Sometime on Friday some one told the marshal
about the prohibition law, and that night he took
possession of Dwyer and O'Dell's playless saloon
and closed it up. By Sunday when the Gulch was
resonant with the pealing of church bells, there was
still no gambling, but all the saloons except the
Dwyer and O'Dell place were running full tilt with
the hard liquor flowing cheerily. Romeo was
thoroughly discouraged and he and Jack O'Dell
and their faro dealer, Frank Du Belois, went down

to Hot Springs. It is characteristic of Deadwood that in spite of the ruin of their business after weeks of annoyance and trouble, O'Dell held no grudge against his partner for his ill-advised interest in the city government.

The Prohibition Enforcement League thought this was a propitious time to poke up its head out of obscurity and announced that it "probably would proceed against the saloons on Monday, December 8." The saloon keepers, however, refused to be alarmed and subsequent proceedings proved their wisdom.

Early in December the gamblers' cases came up before a justice of the peace in Central City. Romeo was absent from the cast of the play that had been built up around him, and Marshal Garr not appearing to prosecute them, the accused men all were discharged and went home, calmly to reopen their little games.

After everything seemed to be quiet and the gambling and prohibition laws again forgotten, some one got out an injunction against the Gem Theater for selling liquor. The bar and the gambling rooms were closed until evening when Johnny Burns with grieved and injured air called the attention of the authorities to the fact that the curtain of the Gem Theater could not go up unless the gambling rooms were opened up again because that was the one and only route by which the performers could reach the stage from their sleeping quarters. They were opened immediately and the injunction was lost.

As for Romeo Dwyer, who had caused all the disturbance and who was not very popular anyway, even in his own profession, he never came back from Hot Springs and the Prohibition Enforcement League faded away. Sol Star, having taught his people what to expect if they opposed him, ceased from troubling, and the saloons and gambling houses resumed their merry, nefarious, and unmolested course up and down the Gulch.

THE GEM VARIETY THEATER AND DANCE HALL.

The best known mining camp theater, at the height of its prosperity in the early eighties. In the carriages are, on the left, Al Swearengen, manager and proprietor, with his wife; and on the right, Johnny Burns, "box-herder."

(*From a contemporary photograph.*)

Sky Pilots of the Hills

Chapter 6

SKY PILOTS OF THE HILLS

N old blanket Indian, sitting pompously in a stiff wooden chair on the shady porch of the French Hotel one hot afternoon in August, told me about the first sky pilot of the Black Hills.

The Man-Who-Feigns-Sleep was in Deadwood to testify in the trial of his son, Eagle Hawk, for the murder of the latter's wife. Squatted around him on the porch were braves and squaws, all in attendance at the court of the Great White Father. Missouri, one of the deputy sheriffs, had taken Irene and me over to the hotel to see them. Indians never were an old story to us. They still were gorgeous in those days with rainbow-hued blankets, paint, beads, and porcupine quills, and in the midst of all the pagan splendor, the large ebony crucifix with its ivory figure, hanging on a chain of bright beads around the neck of The-Man-Who-Feigns-Sleep, attracted our instant, inquiring attention. Missouri asked about it through the interpreter, for like all the old Indians, The-Man-Who-Feigns-Sleep scorned the tongue of the invader.

The crucifix had been presented to his family long ago, he said, by Father DeSmet who had been among the Indians around the Pa-Ha-Sa-Pa more than forty years before and who knew there was

167

Old Deadwood Days

gold in the mountains of the Black Hills. He had discovered a rich vein and covered it up because he did not want the paleface with his long fingers reaching down into the ground for the yellow metal to come among his children and take from them the lands and the traditions of their fathers.

Father DeSmet died the year before the first prospector panned gold in French Creek yet through all the early years he was a vivid living personality. A great gold mine was named for him; it was his memory among the Sioux that brought the demand from their chiefs at the signing of the treaty, that "the black robes be sent among them"; and because of him the glory of the first of the sky pilots goes to the Catholic Church.

When Eagle Hawk was acquitted of the murder charge, The-Man-Who-Feigns-Sleep gave the credit to the miraculous power of the crucifix Father De-Smet had given his family.

"The white man's law is just and good," he said. "Justice does not sleep."

Sky pilot was the name given impartially to every clergyman who came into Deadwood Gulch, where the sky needed pilots. The odds against it in its rivalry with the gold-veined ground and glittering streams were too great. But this very fact was an advantage to the sky pilots. The pioneers gave them more credit for knowing their business than they did mining experts.

"Mining experts!" I heard one old prospector say to another as I passed them where they sat on the stone coping of the First National Bank. "Why those mining experts don't know but what mines grow on trees."

People could not come in from the outside and tell them about their own business which was gold mining in the Hills. They knew about that themselves. But the sky, out beyond the stars and the Italian blue bowl of their vision—that was different. They would take the pilot's word for that.

"Preacher Smith," who walked into Deadwood from Custer one May day in '76 with one of Captain Gardner's freight outfits, was the first sky pilot the Black Hills knew. In less than three months he left an impress on Deadwood that few men have equaled in ten times as many years. He was a tall, kindly looking man, nearly fifty years old but looking less, with dark hair and eyes and a short, dark beard. He built the fires, carried water, and read his Bible in the camps they made at night and noon along the sixty miles he had walked with the Gardner outfit, and then wanted to pay for the privilege, but was refused. That was not the West's way with the pilots. All Captain Gardner had learned about him was that he was a Methodist minister from a little town in Connecticut, had served in the Civil War, and had come to the Hills to preach the Word of God.

In Deadwood he worked during the week at mining, carpentering, timber cutting, wood chopping, and other manual labor. On Sunday he preached in the street. He lived quietly and frugally in a little log cabin he had built himself in the high corner of Mrs. L. C. Miller's yard. Bert Miller told me once he remembered Preacher Smith, a pleasant, quiet man who came and went in the little cabin, but Bert was just a little chap in kilts then and he couldn't recall how he looked. It is Captain Gardner, George Ayers, and McClintock who carry the clearest picture of him in their minds.

On Sunday, August 20, 1876, Preacher Smith started to walk alone through the tall pines down the mountains from Deadwood to preach in Crook City. Before starting he wrote on a rough card that he nailed to his cabin door: "Gone to Crook City to preach and, God willing, will be back at three o'clock." Reports were that the Indians were ugly and the miners urged him not to go.

"This is my protection," he replied, holding up his Bible. One of the miners said he would rather have a cap and ball revolver against the Indians.

"It never has failed me yet," the clergyman insisted, "and I am not afraid to put my trust in it now."

A few miles out of Deadwood Preacher Smith was killed by the Indians. The men of Deadwood Gulch always believed that the Bible would have saved his life if it had "shot quicker." It had saved him from being scalped but the Indians had not seen it nor known who the man was when they killed him.

He was found dead by the roadside and when he was brought back to camp on a load of hay, the whole camp rose to arm itself and go out after the Indians. All dealers in arms and cartridges handed their wares out freely. John Gaston had fifty new needle guns with ammunition that he gave without question to the first men who asked for weapons.

Sky Pilots of the Hills

The sermon Preacher Smith meant to deliver at Crook City was in his pocket, a sermon taken from the text: "By whom we have received grace and apostleship, for obedience to the faith among all nations for His name." More people have read that undelivered sermon than ever would have heard it if it had been preached in Crook City.

"Many ways there are," it proclaimed, "in which we may assist in spreading abroad the story of the Cross." Preacher Smith did it by giving up his life.

When the old Ingleside cemetery was moved in '83 to the table top of Hebrew Hill between White Rocks and the Gulch, a newspaper notice brought a letter from Preacher Smith's daughter Edna in Connecticut to Porter Warner of the *Times* giving further details of her father's life. She said he was the youngest of three brothers all of whom had met violent deaths. He had been expecting to send for his wife and children in the fall of '76 and had been sending them money they never received because the mail carrier of the pony express had been robbed and murdered. The scattered letters had been gathered up later and sent on to the family but they had been rifled of all money. This, she said, had left the family destitute at the time of her father's death but since then she had been teaching in the little town where they lived.

Edna Smith's letter revived all the interest in the old tragedy and Deadwood rose to the privilege of being able to do something for its martyred minister. Money was raised to bring Mrs. Smith and her two daughters to Deadwood where all the people, especially the pioneers of '76, would be their friends.

Old Deadwood Days

Mrs. Tracy donated a beautiful zephyr worsted scarf that Mrs. Kingsley told Mother was worth fifty dollars, and it was raffled off down at the Headquarters saloon at fifty cents a chance for the benefit of the Smith family. It was on exhibition in the window and we all made the most of the opportunity to go and look in a saloon window but we didn't see anything but the scarf. The school board made a place in the public schools for Edna Smith. Marvin Hughitt of the Chicago and Northwestern Railway, sent passes for the whole family as far as Pierre, which was the end of the railroad then, and arrangements were made for bringing them from Pierre to Deadwood by stage.

There was a good deal of correspondence between Porter Warner and Edna Smith and then there was a long delay after which Mr. Warner got a letter from Mrs. Smith, herself an invalid, saying that Edna had been very ill and they would not be able to come. All the money that had been raised was sent to them, but they never were able to make the long journey.

The Congregational was the dramatic pioneer church not only of Deadwood but of all the Black Hills. Built on a firm foundation of bed-rock, it stood at the foot of McGovern Hill just above the place where Deadwood and Whitewood creeks came together—a vantage point that commanded a view of all that part of the town that most needed watching. The first pastor, the Rev. L. P. Norcross, came to Deadwood in November, '76, and held services in Backrus' carpenter shop.

It was in another carpenter shop, unfinished and

open, that Father Lonergan celebrated the first mass one Sunday morning in May, 1877. Curious how they worshipped in carpenter shops, those early Deadwood Christians!

One Sunday night not long before the hour for the Congregational evening service, fire broke out in the Senate saloon. Mr. Norcross, in his miner's clothes had just come back to his cabin near by from a climb through the hills, when he heard the alarm and hurried to the fire. It needed everybody's help and he worked valiantly until after time for his evening service. He went over hurriedly to explain and dismiss whatever congregation might be lingering. The chilly little room was full when he arrived, sooty and disheveled, in his corduroys and high boots. His face and hands were grimy and muddy little icicles clung to his clothes.

"I can't hold service this way," he said after he had explained about the fire.

"Why not?" demanded one of the pillars in a front seat. "We're satisfied, and you don't think the Lord is any less understanding than we are, do you?"

So Mr. Norcross read the chapter about the sheep falling into a pit on the Sabbath day and the service went on.

Once Father Kelly, one of the temporary priests of the Catholic Church, saw a fire on the roof of the Merchants Hotel as he was passing and, taking some salt and a bucket of water went up by himself and put it out.

"It isn't such a bad idea," Father said once, telling the two incidents together, "for the sky pilots to get a reputation for being able to quench fire."

The Congregational Church was completed and opened for worship in July, '77, less than six months after A. W. Hastie, a lawyer, and L. C. Miller, an insurance man, had started out one day to raise money to build a church and collected four hundred dollars in the first hour. It was an unattractive frame building painted a nondescript gray with a crude, temporary belfry perched on the northeast corner to house the old boat bell that Captain Beard, captain on a Missouri River steamboat, had presented to the church. It was a loud old bell and as soon as it was in place one of the workmen pulled the rope to test it and Deadwood's first church bell pealed out its message.

Twenty or thirty men at work on placer claims on Deadwood Creek straightened up from their pans and sluice boxes at the first stroke of the bell, removed their soft hats, and stood at reverent attention until the last ringing echo died away down the gulch. No one of them said a word. None of them mentioned the incident afterwards. A woman living in a log cabin between the placer mines and the church who watched them from her open door while she listened to the first church bell told Mother about it one afternoon, a long time after, when they were making sandwiches down in an empty store building where we were to have a church supper that night.

Everybody used the Congregational Church—Congregationalists, Methodists, Episcopalians, making their hours of service fit into each other.

The Rev. Arthur Cushing Dill came to the Con-

Sky Pilots of the Hills

gregational Church in the early 'eighties, a slight little man under thirty with a zeal and enthusiasm that encompassed not only the upper end of the gulch, Forest Hill, and Ingleside, but reached down and through the badlands into Chinatown, stopping everywhere along the way.

"He's all right," I heard Mr. Kingsley say to Father one cold morning as we all stood around the stove in the back of the church before the service began. "He's all right," reservedly, "the only trouble with him is he's too young."

Father shook his head and smiled. "Never worry about a fault a man is so sure to overcome. He'll get over being too young. That's one thing that's certain."

I suppose he did get over it in time but not while he stayed in Deadwood. He was very young and very enthusiastic during all of his pastorate there. Outstanding in the work he did and perhaps the most long-reaching in its influence, was his Chinese school. Everybody was drafted into teaching a Chinaman one night a week in the little basement of the church. They came in droves and we taught them to read, write, and speak English, all as a substructure for the spiritual instruction Mr. Dill later would impose upon their unsuspecting pagan souls. They all wanted to know English. It was needful in their business of making enough money to go back to China to live out the rest of their lives in peace and plenty among their own people. They brought an old Oriental atmosphere into the church that had not yet lost its newness. They brought us presents too—china, carved ivory, sandalwood, and em-

175

Old Deadwood Days

broidered crêpe. Mr. Dill taught them to sing a
good-night song, and I can see them now, a little
dark group standing out in the night with Mr. Dill
in their midst between the church and Red Creek,
singing in voices not attuned to western melody:
"Good night, ladies. Good night, ladies. Good
night, ladies. We're going to leave you now."

I decided I would be a missionary to China just
as soon as I was old enough and that being some
years away no one took the trouble to discourage
me. So I started in to learn the language at once.
It was nothing to me whether my Chinaman learned
any English or not. I was going to learn Chinese.
I mastered the days of the week and a greeting.
That's as far as I got. The Chinaman fared better.
I think there probably are several Chinamen in
Deadwood, or more likely Canton, who owe the
rudiments of their knowledge of English to Mr.
Dill's Chinese school. A few of them under his
urging joined the church and stayed around in our
lives. They made proud use of the English they
had learned. Yee Murk who was Colonel Steele's
janitor, I recall, communicated with him almost
entirely by letters. He might see the Colonel half
a dozen times a day but when he had anything important to say he wrote a note. One of his classics
read: "Mr. Chicken Pot Pie, he sawem wood. Us
to him two dollars'n a half."

One Christmas while Mr. Dill was in Deadwood
the China boys arranged to give him a present of a
gorgeous tea set including a heavily embroidered
silk cozy for the teapot. Yee Tang, because he was
a leader among them and spoke the best English,

Sky Pilots of the Hills

was chosen to make the presentation speech. Not trusting his own powers of composition, he went to Mr. Elder, a young attorney who was interested in the church and all its works, and asked him to write it for him.

"Put in some nice big words, Mr. Elder," Tang suggested. He wanted to impress both Mr. Dill and the other China boys with his knowledge of English.

"As a slight token of our appreciation of Mr. Dill's indefatigable interest in our people," the presentation speech began. Tang worried with the word "appreciation" for a while and finally mastered it. Then he began on "indefatigable." He stumbled around on that until he got discouraged.

"Say, Mr. Elder," he asked finally, "can't you leave out some of that fat?"

In the late 'eighties the Rev. Alexander McConnell, as dignified and steadfast as his name, came to the Congregational Church. He was so reserved looking with his closely clipped side whiskers, his frock coat, and his high silk hat, as much a part of him as the thoughtful sermons he preached, that one would not have expected the badlands to sense so quickly and accurately his kindly reasonable understanding of them. He had been in Deadwood several years when, early one evening, a messenger came to the parsonage on Centennial avenue, a diffident pale man who did not know Mr. McConnell and seemed to anticipate being rebuffed. He said that Hattie Bell was dying in her castle over on Fink's Flats and wanted Mr. McConnell to come and see her. Certainly. Mr. McConnell would be

177

right over. He not only was sympathetic but friendly. The messenger was puzzled. Did "the reverend" know who Hattie Bell was? Yes, of course he knew who she was. He knew her personally. He had been at her house several times to see girls who were sick or in trouble.

"The doctor says," the man continued haltingly, "that she probably will live till along toward morning, and she'll be wanting you to stay."

"I'll stay just as long as she wants me." And the man went away convinced.

Almost immediately on his heels Mr. McConnell followed with Father, whom he had asked to accompany him. They stayed with Hattie Bell, reading scripture to her as she requested, Mr. McConnell offering a short prayer now and then and talking to her of the journey she was about to take. She died a little before dawn after expressing her gratitude to them both with the courtesy and dignity that made her the sort of woman an editorial writer back in the 'seventies had in mind once when he urged "regulation for the social evil similar to the one they had in Cheyenne." That he said worked admirably. "A monthly fine not only replenishes a depleted city treasury but has a most salutary effect in driving the women of the street out of town or into a house kept by a responsible Madam." Hattie Bell, in her castle on Fink's Flat, was a "responsible Madam."

Father Rosen was a stalwart, untiring man who, through most of the 'eighties, served the parish of St. Ambrose in Deadwood, together with dozens of fledgling parishes around in smaller camps, found

Sky Pilots of the Hills

time to look after innumerable spiritual mavericks, and write a book, "Pa-Ha-Sa-Pa."

One day in the early spring when the roads were almost impassable, he got a call to go to Carbonate Camp where a miner he knew was dying of mountain fever. Before starting in his one-horse buggy he went down to see Mrs. Geis who ran a hotel in the first ward and who was his dependable ally in works of charity and mercy.

"This fellow thinks he's going to die," he told her, "but he may not be as sick as he thinks he is, and if he's able I'm going to bring him back with me. Can you find a place to stow him away, do you think?" This with full knowledge that if she did, she not only would provide food and shelter but adequate nursing.

"The house is pretty full," she said slowly, thinking as she talked. "But I'll find a corner somewhere."

"I'll pay the bill," Father Rosen promised.

"I'll cut it in two," Mrs. Geis countered.

When the priest arrived at the cabin in Carbonate he found his parishioner able to travel and proceeded immediately to help him get into his clothes. He had come to his boots and was discussing with him the advisability of going over to the hotel for a little hot soup to bolster him up on the journey when a wail arose unexpectedly from a bunk in the corner.

"What's the matter with you?" Father Rosen demanded, a surprised emphasis on the pronoun.

"I'm just as sick as he is," the wail articulated, "and I want to go to Deadwood, too. I'll die if I stay here. But I don't belong to no church and nobody cares what happens to me. That's what I get for being a heathen and a sinner."

"Oh, hush up," Father Rosen commanded. "Wait till I get through with this fellow, and I'll help you get dressed and take you along."

He was hunting for the second patient's trousers when from a third corner in the dark there came a long husky groan. The priest looked questioningly from one to the other of the first two men. "What's this? Another sick sinner wanting to be saved?"

The two men explained that the third was their partner and he had mountain fever, too.

"Well, how many more?" patiently. "You know I can't take a whole shift in my buggy. It's supposed to carry two."

They assured him there were no more and after a good deal of difficulty he got the three of them dressed and fed and crowded into his buggy. Over rough roads, up hill and down, and along an occasional shelving way, he brought them at last to Mrs. Geis and her comfortable "corner." She didn't mind. She wasn't even surprised. She long since had grown accustomed to Father Rosen's charities.

The infinite patience of Father Rosen was something no one could fathom who did not know his next door neighbor. Henrico Livingstone was so quarrelsome and so insistent about her mining rights that once the residents of City Creek called a mass meeting to "protest against her destruction of their homes." Father Rosen was getting along all right with her until he decided to build a stable and, having hired a man to excavate a place for it on his own lot back of his house between it and Henrico's cabin, took his horse and buggy and drove out of town on priestly business. The man he left behind went to work and was making rapid progress when a woman's harsh voice stopped him. He turned around with a shovelful of dirt in his hands and looked into the barrel of a Winchester with the gaunt figure of Henrico behind it.

"Quit that or I'll shoot."

The man quit that and went down town and had her arrested. The arrest happened at recess time. Horace Clark saw the marshal going up the hill and ballyhooed the event to the rest of us. We were lined up a dozen deep along the back fence when the marshal and Henrico came walking quietly down the hill together. One boy on the fence made a rude remark and the marshal told him to shut up, adding that if he heard anything more he'd take some boys along with him. Nobody tried any more smart sallies.

Henrico being brought into court and confronted with the charge of having pulled a gun on a man because he was dumping dirt on her property, claimed that he "was covering up her vein of ore." The judge ordered her released on her own recognizance, but she wouldn't go. She insisted on going to jail. She said she knew a woman once who was arrested and let out on bail and while she was out she was robbed and murdered. Bail was no safe thing to be out on, according to Henrico. The judge and the lawyers and the marshal all argued with her, but go to jail she would. They could not keep her out.

The next day she sent up to her cabin for her own bedding and some clothes and proceeded to make herself comfortable. She did not leave until she had been tried and acquitted and had come to a friendly arrangement with Father Rosen who agreed to have the dirt from the excavation thrown somewhere else. He wanted a stable but only if it could be built without blood and violence.

Rev. R. H. Dolliver of the Methodist Church was the only sky pilot who ever saw Deadwood as an up-to-date Sodom and Gomorrah and spoke of what he saw in his cursory surface glance. Genial and kindly in his everyday life, he rose up in his pulpit when he first arrived and thundered against "the gods of Deadwood." He said they were "King Faro, Prince Stud Poker, Bacchus, and Gambrinus." Female depravity was rampant in our depraved town, according to him, and the bar—meaning the lawyers—and the press used their power and their energies for the protection and encouragement of all this vice.

The papers called his attention courteously to the fact that the reverend gentleman had not been long enough in Deadwood to know all about the place and its people, and that when he became acquainted with us he might like us better and think more highly of us. In the meantime wouldn't it be kindly and Christian to suspend judgment? Mr. Dolliver read the criticisms and accepted the suggestions.

Dr. Clough who came as pastor of the Methodist

Sky Pilots of the Hills

Church and later served the Black Hills as presiding elder, made no mistakes of understanding. He knew perfectly well that in that town of clear contrasts there still was "so much of bad in the best of us, and so much of good in the worst of us," that he hesitated to "draw the line where God has not." He inaugurated the setting aside of the back pews for those outside his own or any other pastor's flock. His own people were not permitted to sit in those three back pews at all on Sunday night. They were filled with men to whom church services were either a novelty or an echo of forgotten habits. They were gamblers, bartenders, sometimes just weary loafers. They came in singly, by twos, or in small groups after the first hymn had begun, and they slipped out just before the benediction. There never was an empty seat and it became necessary to increase the number of those reserved.

"I told them they could do that," Dr. Clough explained to his family and to the men of the church. "They don't want to talk to people and have people talking at them. They'll quit coming if we don't let them alone. They come for the service and the sermon. Not such a bad idea for the consideration of some people who think they're better than my back-pew friends."

The Episcopal Church through the stagecoach days had a changing broken line of rectors unified and dominated by the fragile figure and powerful personality of Bishop Hare. No one of them ever stayed long enough to make a deep impress on either the church or the town until the new era of the 'nineties came in and brought with it Mr. Ware of

183

the vivid charm and the long bright-starred pastorate. Preceding him came Mr. Molyneux, slim,
dark, and ritualistic, who played the piano like a
professional and was much in demand at dinner
parties. I would have thought his life was all music
and incense if it had not been for the time Mrs.
McPherson and Mrs. Cheairs and I went with him
to a wedding at Carbonate and made the detour
to a cabin down by the mill. Mrs. McPherson
had offered to drive him out and had suggested
that I might play the wedding march, so we
all started off gayly. At the turn of the road
leading down into the camp a man on horseback
halted us.

"I beg your pardon," he said to Mr. Molyneux,
"but I noticed your round collar and I thought perhaps you would come and see a man who is dying
down here in his cabin."

So we drove with the man riding like an escort
beside us, and Mrs. McPherson and Mrs. Cheairs
and I waited outside in the carriage while Mr. Molyneux went inside. We tried to be as grave and de-
corous as the occasion demanded and our high
spirits made possible. Two men in corduroys and
high boots came along and went in while we waited,
speaking pleasantly but solemnly to us as they
passed.

When Mr. Molyneux came out and climbed in
beside Mrs. McPherson his face was a study in
seriousness and suppressed mirth. He said the man,
whose name was Sam Houston, a well known miner,
was dead. We drove along up through the spicy
pine trees, no one saying anything until we came up

Sky Pilots of the Hills

on the ridge where we could look down on the camp. The wedding to which we were going was at the other end of the Gulch.

Mr. Molyneux turned a little in his seat so that his voice could reach us all without being raised. "I think I'll tell you this," he said, and we were all attention.

"Before I arrived, Sam Houston, who knew he was going to die, had sent for his two partners. Perhaps you noticed them come in. He asked them to sit down, one on each side of his bed, and then we all sat around, perfectly still. Finally one of them spoke to him:

" 'Was there something you wanted to say to us, Sam? Anything you want us to do?'

"Sam shook his head. 'No, nothing.'

" 'We'd be glad to do anything.'

"He shook his head again.

"There was a long pause and then: 'You didn't have anything on your mind, Sam, when you sent for us?'

" 'Yes,' in a whisper, 'I wanted to die like our Lord—between two thieves!' "

Mr. Molyneux turned away from us all with a little gesture that dared us to smile. "There," he said, indicating a little frame house standing toward the top of the hill a little apart, "that's where we're going. That's where our wedding is." He never mentioned Sam Houston again.

Once at Mrs. McPherson's when the bishop was there, long after Mr. Molyneux was gone, Mrs. Cheairs said she wondered if Mr. Molyneux understood how seemingly trifling these old prospectors

185

could be, yet how really serious and reverent at heart.

The bishop said he was coming to believe that no life was long enough for any one man to understand another. "All we can do," he said, "is to give what we can of our meager, hard-won wisdom and let the other people work things out for themselves. Even the Indians."

An old squaw down on the Pine Ridge reservation told me the story of the bishop and the little Ogallala girl once when I was visiting the Brennans while Mr. Brennan was the Indian agent there. Old Nellie, they called her, and I can see her now huddled down in a low chair beside the piano where I had been trying to pick out the old Indian melodies she crooned. She had learned English from the Indian fighters of the United States Army, and, telling me rambling little stories about her people, she came at last to the story of this girl who could not adapt herself to the ways of the white man.

Lucy Lone Eagle, she said, went to the government school and was confirmed by Bishop Hare at the agency in the little white church with the cross —she and half a dozen other Indian girls and boys. She wasn't happy when she came home. Nellie didn't know why. Perhaps there was a white man. You never could tell. When it came time to get ready for the ghost dance, many Indian women came to the Lone Eagle tepee to make ghost shirts. They were primitive looking garments. Old Nellie had brought one to show me. It was made of yellowish unbleached muslin, cut in straight crude lines as a little child fashions its doll garments and

Sky Pilots of the Hills

was decorated with red and yellow paint made from the clays along the White River. Lucy joined them in their work but her mother stopped her.

"My daughter," she said, "you must not dance the ghost dance. You belong to the white man's church. You believe in the white man's religion. You must not dance the ghost dance. That, as you know, is a rite of the Indian religion. It does not belong to the church of the paleface. You cannot dance. You must not come."

The girl folded up her work and put it away, but that afternoon she went into the agency where the bishop was making a visitation. She took her cross and her prayer book and laid them on the table before him in the study back of the little white church, and quietly renounced the new and untried faith. Then she went back to her own people and the ghost dance.

Bishop Hare did not try to reason with her. He had had long years of experience with the Indians and he had infinite patience and a great love for them.

"You expect too much," he told a young priest on the reservation once. "The Indians are coming in slowly. Look at our Indian churches, and the number of our native priests. It took three thousand years to civilize Europe. We can't expect to Christianize the Indian in ten."

So he let the little Ogallala girl follow her heart and her traditions and go back to her own people and the ghost dance. He knew that nothing he could say then could hold her. No man had any power to prevent the tragedy that followed.

Old Deadwood Days

That was the Sioux last ghost dance. It ended in a great war and was forever forbidden by the Great Father at Washington. It was the wildest, maddest ghost dance the tribe had ever known.

At the close of the dance, Lucy Lone Eagle dropped dead.

The agency doctor, Mr. Brennan told me, called it heart failure. She had danced furiously for three days.

But old Nellie, crouched in her chair in a dusky corner beside the piano told me in a husky whisper:

"She gave up the white man's religion, went back to her father's gods and the ghost dance, and the God of the white man struck her dead."

The Mother of the Badlands

Chapter 7

THE MOTHER OF THE BADLANDS

A BRILLIANT bit of scarlet awning over a little space of sidewalk just above the Main street deadline. A stand of yellow oranges, pink peaches, purple plums, and blue and white grapes. A fussy, busy peanut roaster. And in the midst a tired shabby old woman dozing between times in her big old-fashioned wooden rocker. To the casual passer-by, it was a splash of color wedged in between dull blind-drawn saloons. To those who knew—Mrs. Hayes' little business was the kind heart of the badlands, a house of refuge for tawdry troubled women and nameless forgotten children.

Back of the sidewalk shop in two cluttered little rooms of a flimsy board shack that some indifferent carpenter had thrown up in an idle moment, Mrs. Hayes lived, kept her stock at night, and when the weather drove her inside, still did business. I always suspected that she lived chiefly on overripe fruit and beer.

My friendship with her began suddenly and strangely one day when in a moment of reckless extravagance I stopped to buy peaches. My mother thought peaches were rosy globes of ambrosia known only to Paradise and an Ohio farm. Father and the General thought they were more like edible gold nuggets—the size they used to get over in Potato Gulch. But we all occasionally let a necessity slide and bought them for Mother. We had to buy an ample supply for the whole family or she didn't care for them.

Mrs. Hayes knew who I was and told me that day while she picked out the most luscious of her peaches that she had come west to Kansas as a maid in the family of my uncle James and had been married at his house. With that background, she became at once a sort of liege-woman in the house of Bennett and aroused in me a strong sense of responsibility and obligation. No one in the family had known this. Father and the General, however, knew other things about her equally interesting and more dramatic. They remembered her husband and they had known Paul Gentzes, the man who killed him back in the 'seventies and spent the rest of his life in bitter regret and material amende.

The two men had quarreled in a saloon over a poker game and Gentzes had thrown a beer glass at Hayes, breaking his skull and killing him instantly. A jury acquitted Gentzes on the ground that he had not intended to commit murder and that a beer glass was not a deadly weapon. It seemed to have accomplished the same results in that case but anyway they let him go. As long as he lived he provided for Mrs. Hayes and spent the balance of the profits from his brewery on the wherewithal to drown his very real remorse. When he died there was nothing left to bequeath to the widow of the man he inadvertently had killed, and it was then that Mrs. Hayes opened her fruit stand. It moved about

The Mother of the Badlands

town for a while and finally came to its permanent yet transient-appearing location on lower Main street. She built up a trade and in the business of living and of selling fruit, did the best she could which after all wasn't so bad, everything considered, and little by little drew about her graying head a changing circle of perplexed troubles.

Under her bright awning were gathered the sordid tragedies and helpless griefs of the badlands. Homeless, fatherless little children of careless mothers found safe harbor in that vivid patch of fruit merchandise. Futile, wretched young girls brought their heart-breaks and their bewilderments into the seclusion of the disordered little shack. Mrs. Hayes was close enough to them to understand. I learned about the badlands from her. I bought all the fruit I could and made all the excuses possible to stop and talk to her. If ever, on a hurried errand I considered passing her place after she was up and around, such thought was frustrated by her beckoning old forefinger and her command to "Come 'ere." I never could refuse. Her call meant another act in the raw badlands drama that centered around her and her poverty-stricken shack.

Mrs. Hayes' working day began in the middle of the afternoon. Her trade came chiefly from the badlands that didn't know there was such a thing as a morning, and stayed awake and active until long after midnight. She never closed as long as any badlanders sauntered about the street. She sat in her big old rocker and when business was dull, dozed. That might just as well be in the warm drowsy quiet of the afternoon as in the noisy middle

Old Deadwood Days

of the night. People who were unkind said she dozed because she was drunk. Sometimes she heard the gossip and once she told me about it.

"They say I get drunk," she said indignantly after she had summoned me confidentially close. "Did you ever see me drunk?"

I assured her I had not.

"Well," she replied triumphantly, "if I get drunk I'm smarter than any of the men because I can always attend to business. There ain't any of the men can get drunk and attend to business, is there? Do you know any? No. When a man gets drunk— 'tend to business? Huh."

She was right about that. You always could wake her up and make a purchase.

She was a very shabby, ragged old woman and the looks of her offended my sense of noblesse oblige, remembering that she once had been a maid in a branch of our family, so I asked my mother if she didn't have some old frock she could fix up for her.

Mother didn't share my sense of personal responsibility for Mrs. Hayes but she always had something for anyone in need. In those days she wore morning dresses that she called wrappers but there was nothing *negligee* about their neat trim fit and the way they buttoned primly up under her chin. Of course they trailed, but everything trailed in the 'eighties. She had one made of sateen with a bright green figure in it that she was just about to discard when I made my plea. She mended it all up, had it washed and ironed, and I bore it triumphantly down to my *protégée*. Mrs. Hayes was just as pleased as I had expected her to be. It had been a long time

The Mother of the Badlands

since she had owned a garment that was clean and whole. No one ever had seen her look so nice and I was filled with smug satisfaction.

Several days later Mother was standing in the bay window watering her fuchsias and geraniums when she called me to come quickly. I was not as prompt as I should have been so I missed what she saw. The view from the window commanded an alley that ran back of the houses on Main street. Among them was Mrs. Hayes' poor little shack next door to a two-story brick building that housed "Pete's Place."

"I never thought," Mother said with one of her characteristic dramatic gestures, "that I would ever come to this. I looked down in the alley just now and I saw my old green wrapper coming out of the back door of Pete's Place. There was a bucket of something carried along——"

"Beer," I enlightened her. "By to-night it will be all over town that Mrs. Bennett has taken to rushing the can at Pete's Place."

She pretended not to know what I was talking about and that night at dinner told the family the story of her demoralized green wrapper. Halle said that was the difference between Mother's charities and mine. Mother, she said, always was doing for the worthy poor, but mine not only were unworthy but thoroughly disreputable. Not only Mother, but Father, the General, Robbie, and Gaylord, all agreed with her. They all said in their own ways and phrases that whenever I held out my hand to help anybody over a mud hole, I just shook hands with them and got my own hand dirty and

Old Deadwood Days

they stayed where they were. They couldn't be pulled out. Mother had only to speak to hers and they came up out of their shallow little puddles into which an unkind fate had pushed them, onto the nice dry place beside her.

They cited as an illustration the family down in the first ward who belonged to our church and had fallen on lean ways because the father and mother had both been sick. Mother went down to see them and made over our clothes for the children and got Father to find the man a job, and the children came to Sunday school in Halle's old blue coat and my outgrown red dress and they were very nice and neat and well-behaved. We never saw any of our old clothes down around the back door of Pete's Place. They were a most worthy family.

Yes of course they were and anybody who heard of their plight would help them out. But no one ever had cared at all what kind of duds old Mrs. Hayes had to walk the alley in until I took an interest. And she had her little crowded place full of lame ducks all the time, and here was Mother begrudging her a little comfort out of Pete's Place while she was wearing her green wrapper.

Mother resented that. She said she begrudged her nothing, and she had another old wrapper I could give Mrs. Hayes if she needed it, but she thought any woman was better off without beer.

"Come here," Mrs. Hayes said one day, crooking her forefinger to beckon me. "See this child?"

A round-faced pleasant little girl not more than three years old, sat on a stool on the sidewalk and smiled at us both impartially.

The Mother of the Badlands

"Her mother ain't come for her yet, and here it's getting toward dark. She left her here about this time yesterday and I kept her all night. And now all day, too. Jennie's drunk. That's what she is. W'addaya think o' that? Get drunk and forget about her baby. W'addaya think o' that?"

"She knew you'd take care of her," I ventured.

"She didn't know nothin'. A woman don't know nothin' when she's drinking."

I wondered. Mrs. Hayes always knew enough to take care of the forsaken babies. The beer she brought from Pete's Place never interfered with her mothering. She fed them what she had, was kind to them, and along toward morning took them to bed with her. They fared better—those badland babies—with Mrs. Hayes than with their own irresponsible mothers into whom she tried hard to instill some sense of duty.

I was a valuable colleague in those days because my father was county judge, the guardian of Mrs. Hayes' little waifs, and easy of appeal because he had a deep-rooted aversion to institutions for children. He would go more than half way to meet almost any kind of a parent. The only ones that baffled him utterly were Blonde May and the father and mother of Julia and Willie.

Blonde May was a thin, frightened, faded-looking woman who never apparently had been able to cope with life as she found it. I would have supposed she would be very easily influenced and controlled. Probably she was where her child was not concerned. She sat back in a dark corner of Mrs. Hayes' front room holding her five-year-old daughter tight in

197

her arms and cried hopelessly. A policeman had told her the court was going to take Pearlie away and send her to the Children's Home.

Near the door Mrs. Hayes stood talking with a priest when I came by and she called me in consultation. He was temporarily at St. Ambrose's Church and I didn't know him. He wanted to have the child sent down to St. Martin's Academy at Sturgis where the mother could go and see her sometimes, but he had been in court and he verified the policeman's statement. The disposition of May's little girl had not been made official yet but it was positive. They were all very sad.

"May's down on her luck," Mrs. Hayes explained to me as she wiped her eyes with a loose end of her sleeve and spoke in low tones that May was not supposed to hear. "You know May drinks and she takes dope." Suddenly she turned around and raised her voice. "What do you do it for, May? Why don't you quit?"

May whimpered and said she did try but if they took Pearlie away from her there wouldn't be any use in anything.

In my arrogant young righteousness I suggested that if she would behave herself probably they wouldn't take Pearlie away from her.

The priest who had been saying nothing turned to me and asked if I thought there would be any use in my speaking to my father. He said he would be responsible for seeing that the little girl was sent to St. Martin's. So he and I went up to Father's office and told him how things were and he said if the priest would assume the responsibility for the child

The Mother of the Badlands

and see that she was sent to the convent, he was willing to turn the child over to him. Also, he didn't care at all how often the mother went to see her. Father was very glad to have it settled that way and the kindly priest and I went back to break the glad tidings to May and Mrs. Hayes. They both wept with joy. We explained things carefully to Pearlie and, everybody else being satisfied, she accepted the arrangements cheerfully, too. The priest took her and her mother to Sturgis the next day and everything was all right—for a while.

Father came home one night and waited until dessert before he told me his news.

"What do you suppose has happened to your little protégée at St. Martin's?"

"Dear me, she isn't dead or anything? May hasn't killed her and committed suicide?"

"Nonsense. They've run away. Your friend, May, went down to see her little girl, asked to take her down town to get her some shoes, and disappeared. She didn't take the stage, she had been in none of the shoe stores, and no one in Sturgis has seen her. The valley must just have cracked and swallowed them up."

"Bear Butte came down and ate 'em," Robbie suggested and Father thought that was quite as likely as anything else.

"Do you care?" I asked Father.

No, he said he didn't, as long as they stayed out of Lawrence county and people didn't bother him with complaints about them.

Mother said she thought May Whoever-she-was did exactly right. It was her child, wasn't it? "If

199

anyone took a child of mine away from me," she said with her eyes on her plate, "it would be over my dead body."

Father thought that was going a little too far in defiance of the law. "If the proceedings were legal," throwing her a glare that she didn't see because she still was looking at her plate, "they'd put you in jail if you tried——"

"They couldn't," she interrupted him still without raising her eyes, "I'd be dead."

Father got up and left the table and I never heard of May and Pearlie again. I asked Mrs. Hayes once or twice but she had heard nothing. She thought that "if May wanted the kid so bad mebbe she'd brace up and behave herself and take care of her." Father and I thought she was a good deal of an optimist.

I first saw Willie Milton one day when I was standing out in front of Mrs. Hayes' bartering for oranges that were small and not very tempting. She was willing to sell them to me for almost anything if I would just listen to her troubled tale about the policeman who said she was drunk the night before. I said it was an outrageous libel and got a dozen oranges for thirty cents. While she was hunting for a bag to put them in, a small boy of seven or eight, shabby, neglected looking, and one-eyed, came dancing up the street as gayly and confidently as though he were the Prince Charming in his protected childhood, and as gracefully as though he were a dancer at the court of the Czar.

He stopped to call Mrs. Hayes' attention to the silver he was jingling in his pockets that looked too

The Mother of the Badlands

ragged to be trusted with riches, and this was a loud jingle he had, speaking authoritatively of silver dollars. Nothing like that could be made with quarters and dimes. He said he had been dancing down in the Growler saloon and some big mining men were there and gave him all this money. He rolled his one eye so that I wondered if he could see out of it and told Mrs. Hayes that he thought he'd quit running errands for "the girls." They never gave him more than a dime. He could make more money dancing.

Mrs. Hayes said it was awful the way his mother let him run around the girls' rooms to do their errands, and dancing in saloons wasn't much better. She said he hardly ever went to school and he didn't eat regular or learn anything. "It's awful," she said with a hard-drawn sigh, "how some women let their children go."

It was the next night at dinner that Father said a complaint had been made to him about a woman named May Milton who lived in the badlands and had a boy, Willie, who needed looking after. Donovan, the policeman, said May had been a dancer at the Gem but she got sick a few months ago and hadn't been able to dance. She lived as she could which seemed to be a polite way of saying that her manner of life was not at all what it should be. She would be glad, however, to live differently and look after her child if she could get work or help from the county or something. She thought she might do plain sewing. Father was sure the county would give her a little help now if she would show a disposition to get her boy out of his present environment. Father had sent for her to come and see him but Donovan said her excuse, that she was not able, was perfectly legitimate. Father wished that Mother would go down to see her and talk to her. He said she could take me along, and Donovan would meet us down on lower Main street and go with us so that we wouldn't get into any more unpleasantness than was necessary.

Donovan saw us from afar off and came to meet us. He apologized a little for the sort of place he was taking us into but Mother said that was all right. Her husband had asked her, she said with shoulders back, chin up, and eyes down, to go and see the woman. She had not expected to find her in pleasant surroundings. "My daughter," she explained further as she saw his glance shift to me, "is all right anywhere as long as she is with me."

Donovan led us up a dark debilitated stairway that obviously had begun life in the open and acquired its cover as a mantle for its older, wickeder years. He opened a morose old door at the top leading into a dark hall that ran crosswise through the middle of the building, and knocked on the first door to the right. No answer. He lifted up his authoritative voice as he repeated the knock.

"May! Oh, May, get up and get dressed. There's some ladies here to see you."

This elicited a sort of mumble from within which I didn't understand, but Donovan did.

"Well, you have to see them whether you want to or not. It's the judge's wife and daughter. He sent them. Get your clothes on quick and open the door."

The Mother of the Badlands

"They don't get up very early down here," the officer felt called upon to explain to Mother, it being then well along in the afternoon.

We stood over against the farther wall and waited. A rough-looking man came out of the room and went down the protesting stairs. Finally the door opened a little way and a bedraggled woman in a soiled old kimona, with her towsled hair twisted up in an emergency knot, invited us in with more graciousness and cordiality than I had expected. The room was small, cheap, and most disorderly. It had two windows that would have looked down on Main street if they had not worn thick dark blinds. May raised one blind a little way and a pale reflection of the glorious Black Hills sunshine, that would be splashing all over Forest Hill now, came in and did what it could. May swept some clothes off a couple of chairs that she offered us and went and sat down on her unmade bed. She offered no apologies of any kind for anything.

"You've come about Willie?" she began. "The judge ain't going to take him away from me? Jus' think, Mrs. Bennett, if it was your child. Have you got any boys?" She threw me a glance that put girls in an inferior class that could just as well be given away as not. But she had struck the right chord with Mother.

"Yes," Mother said quietly. "I have two boys and two girls and I would not give up any one of them, but neither would I," with a glance around that included the room, the woman, and her manner of life, "bring them up in any such way as this."

"What would you do if you didn't have any

husband or any money and was too sick to work?"

Never having considered such a combination of contingencies, Mother had no answer ready and anyway this wasn't getting us anywhere. We had come to find out what could be done about Willie. So Mother ignored the question.

"My husband told me to tell you," she said instead, "that if you would move away from here to some more suitable place, do what work you could—I think he said you could do plain sewing—see that Willie goes to school regularly and does not run errands for the women down here nor dance in the saloons—that if you will agree to all this, he will get some money for you from the county until you are able to take care of yourself and Willie. But you have to promise to do this and then do it, or the court will take your little boy away from you. If anyone threatened to take one of my little boys away from me, I would crawl on my knees and scrub if that were the alternative."

May was watching Mother closely and somehow vaguely she seemed to recognize the woman who had been sheltered and cared for all her life, and somewhere in her dulled mind a spark of resentment flickered. What she said in a whining voice was:

"It's a lot o' trouble to take care of a kid."

"I know it is," Mother agreed. "I have four and while I don't have to provide for them, I find it a lot of trouble just taking care of them. But I don't quit trying. Do you want them to relieve you of the trouble of taking care of yours? Do you want them to take your boy away?"

Mother rose with great dignity and I followed

her example as well as I could. "What shall I tell my husband?" she asked. "What will you do?"

The woman crumpled down on her disorderly bed. "Tell the judge," in a thin little voice, "that I'll do what he says—anything he says—if he just won't take Willie away from me."

Donovan was encouraging when we met him at the foot of the stairs. He thought May would do what she said she would. Father, too, was inclined to be sanguine and immediately set to work the machinery to provide temporary county funds for May and Willie while Donovan was finding a place outside the badlands for them to live. But things didn't move fast enough for May. A few days later she rapped on the kitchen door while I was making salad for dinner and asked if she couldn't get some money from the county right away. She said there was a man was wanting to take care of her. He'd take care of Willie, too. He was like that, and he was waiting.

"Well, just wait a day or two longer," I urged her. I gave her a little money and assured her everything would be all right if she would just be a little patient. "Just wait a day or two," I insisted, and she promised and went away.

Things turned out better in the end than any of us had dared to hope. May and Willie moved into the decent little place that Donovan found, and stayed there. Willie went to school and his mother did a little sewing. What else she did, I don't know. Nobody cared as long as she kept the boy in school and in presumably respectable surroundings with her. They never were a county charge or cause of complaint again. I could turn my interested attention to other wards of the fruit stand and county court and sometimes poke into corners where the court was not concerned.

Old Man Whitney, gambler, bartender, and prospector, died in his cabin at Garden City and with him at the end was the woman called Lou. She had been there only through the summer. The old man had many friends, men in all walks of life, and women in only one. They arranged immediately for an elaborate Christian burial.

I didn't know Whitney. I would have known nothing about his death and funeral if I had not met Mrs. Hayes in Lowe's Bee Hive Store, and helped her buy a crêpe-trimmed black frock and a little black bonnet swathed in yards upon yards of heavy black crêpe veiling for the woman called Lou. She had known Lou for a long time and was glad to do her a service but, as we fingered the quality of the goods in the dress and helped Miss Lyon, the dressmaker, figure how the crêpe should go on to take the place of the satin trimming, and measured the length the veil should be, Mrs. Hayes talked about Lou and she had left her few shreds of character when our shopping for her was done. But Lou felt bad about Whitney, she said. The girls out that way and some in town who were Lou's particular friends had bought black dresses and hats. They were going to stand by Lou, Mrs. Hayes said, and Lou, it seems, did not propose that Whitney should lack for mourners.

Arrangements were made with Dr. Clark of the Methodist Church to conduct the services, and the

The Mother of the Badlands

undertaking parlors were crowded. Down in the front row of chairs, surrounded by her black-garbed friends who cried sympathetically and continuously, Lou sobbed bitterly under her heavy veils. Everybody heard and everybody noticed her. Dr. Clark looked toward her occasionally and apparently was sympathetically impressed with her grief.

In the back of the room I was edged into a little triangle between the General with whom I had come much against his will, Mr. Remer who was much amused at my being there, and a big man they said was Red Forrester. After helping buy the mourning garments I certainly had a right to go to the funeral. So many people cried and cried so loud that I cried too and the General kept getting madder and madder at me. Several times he suggested that I go home, but I stayed on. I was getting a sad sentimental pleasure out of Dr. Clark's sermon as he dwelt on the virtues of the dead man whom he had not known at all. He was using what had been told him, and adding to it his deep, sympathetic love of his fellow men—a love that never considered creed, condition, or conduct.

"And now," he said in conclusion, "what shall we say for the heart-broken widow? the woman who has stood beside him through all his changes of fortune—" he turned toward the sable-veiled woman whose shoulders shook with the violence of her woe, "and is now left without the love and the comradeship——"

Red Forrester had reached the limit of his patience. He hurled a sacrilegious oath across the top of my head at the General and Remer as he turned to go out. "Blankety Blank," he swore in profound disgust, "wouldn't that cork you?"

I stuffed my handkerchief in my mouth and the half strangled giggle that escaped might have been taken for a sympathetic sob. Much to the General's relief, I followed Red outside. I couldn't help remembering some of the things Mrs. Hayes had told me about Lou.

On the edge of the sidewalk, Red Forrester was waiting to follow his old friend to Mount Moriah. When he saw me he took off his hat. "You'll excuse me, Miss, for the language I used. But Lou! Heart-broken widow, indeed! That old harrigan!"

I went on home and tried to give my mother a conservative account of my afternoon excursion before the General reached her with a complaint about my conduct. She was very much displeased with me, however. I couldn't fix the facts up in any way that made her think that Old Man Whitney's funeral was any place for her young daughter to be. And I left out a lot about Lou at that. She said I was to stay away from funerals in the future, and I was quite willing. It wasn't often they were so entertaining. So I went back to Mrs. Hayes and her little black lambs for drama.

The only children in that dusky flock who had regularly married parents were Julia and Willie Hanson. And they were the most neglected of them all. They came up out of the depths of the badlands to Mrs. Hayes alone and of their own accord, always with the same story. Their mother had not been home for days and they had neither fire nor food. There always was a hot blaze in Mrs. Hayes' little

The Mother of the Badlands

stove on cold days, food of a sort in her makeshift cupboard, and a kindly welcome. Mrs. Hanson provided none of these. She was so loose in her morals that she fairly fell in fragments, and nothing ever lived, not even a fox in captivity, that knew as little about maternal obligations. Even Father realized her failure at mothering and spent his time trying to instill some sense of parental responsibility into the children's father who lived somewhere down around Sturgis and had been his client at intervals. Every now and then Father would get the careless parent up into his office and talk to him. The conversation which varied but little from time to time, was in this wise:

"You shouldn't have gone and left them," very sternly. "A man has obligations to his family that he cannot shirk."

"Well," unhappily, "I can't live with that woman. No man could. She's the toughest old trollop——"

"Well it's a fine sort of man you are to go off and leave little children with a woman like that. Now in the first place you have to give me some money for them. They're ragged and hungry. You ought to be ashamed of yourself. Have you seen them? Then you'll have to make arrangements for taking care of them, or I'll send them to the Children's Home at Sioux Falls."

This interview took place periodically, always with the same results. Hanson would leave a little money with Father, promise to arrange things so he could have the children with him, and then go away and stay until Father sent for him again.

When Father was convinced that he could do

nothing with "that old scalawag," as he called him, he sent for Mrs. Hanson to come up and see him. Needless to say, she paid no attention to his informal summons. So Bill Remer who was sheriff then, went after her. She lived in a battered bit of a board shack on the side of the hill in the lower part of town. It never had been much of a success as a house and years of neglect had reduced it to the level of its tenant. Mrs. Hanson's house was as disreputable as she was. The flimsy, narrow front porch had become so decrepit that the steps leading up to it had grown utterly discouraged and had fallen down on their job—literally, away down to the bottom where they had started rather feebly but hopefully a long time ago. What was the use of leading people up to a porch that was going to collapse with them when you got them there?

The sheriff clambered up the side hill and approached a window that apparently was used for entrance and exit, and looking in cautiously saw Mrs. Hanson rocking vigorously back and forth in a wooden chair that had lost one rocker, probably in a fight, and looked as though it would throw its occupant gleefully and maliciously as soon as it caught her off guard.

"Good morning, Mrs. Hanson," the sheriff said politely through the window.

The woman stopped her perilous rocking and leaned forward. "Come in here," she invited threateningly. "Come in here, you——"

He didn't hear what he was because he stepped on a mean rock just then that took a bunch of earth with it and rolled down hill so suddenly that he had

The Mother of the Badlands

to change his footing. This brought him nearer the window.

"No," he said courteously. "No, I won't come in. You come and go up town with me," ingratiatingly. "The judge wants to see you. He wants to talk to you."

The sheriff told Father that her reply to that invitation was a voluble and lurid statement of what she thought of the judge, the sheriff, and all other court officials, just what sort of ancestry they had according to her absolute knowledge, and where and how she was certain they would spend eternity, with a few highly colored remarks that had no bearing at all on the case, thrown in for good measure.

She repeated her inhospitable invitation to the sheriff to come in through her window, but he again declined. She told some one afterwards that "if that big sheriff had just put his head in her window she'd have knocked his block off." He had suspected some such intent at the time.

"You'd better come with me," he coaxed as though he were trying to overcome a lady's objection to the weather. "I told you the judge wants to talk to you. That's all. I've a team and buggy down here at the foot of the hill and I'll drive you up to his office." He made no mention of the deputy who waited also with the horses and buggy.

Mrs. Hanson, continuing her pleasant manner, picked up a wooden bench and threw it at him. He ducked below the window and as he righted himself again he saw Julia and Willie coming up the hill. They gave him a new idea of strategy in his losing battle. He made a rush, gathered them screaming and wriggling one under each arm, threw them into his buggy, and climbed over the wheel as the horses started on a run up the street.

Hearing the terrified shrieks of her offspring, Mrs. Hanson awoke to a sudden and violent interest in them. As the sheriff, his deputy, and the screaming children drove up the street like a stampede of cattle, the woman pursuing with speed and great noise started a perambulating and growing commotion in her wake. Up in the vicinity of Wall street, old Mrs. Hayes, hearing the hubbub, rushed out on the sidewalk and realizing when she saw the sheriff and his deputy that the law had things in hand, tried to head off the mad mother as she rared up the street. She might just as well have called, "nice doggy," to a grizzly with a grievance.

At the dead-line corner a quiet but stubborn yoke of oxen insisted on walking sideways and delayed the sheriff's progress so that when he turned down the alley toward Sherman street, Mrs. Hanson was near enough to recognize her advantage. The sheriff did not see her again and was congratulating himself on having lost her when she faced him at the Lee street crossing, a mad, utterly animal thing fighting without reason for her young.

"Jump out," he ordered his deputy, "and hold that woman till I get to the courthouse with the children."

Jumping over the wheels of a buggy drawn by plunging horses was easy enough, but holding that woman was something else.

The sheriff fixed little Julia with firm stern eyes. "You sit perfectly still," he said in a voice that

Main Street, Deadwood, in gala array for the Fourth of July celebration of 1888.
Inset of JUDGE GRANVILLE G. BENNETT from a late photograph.

The Mother of the Badlands

threatened mysterious but dire catastrophe if she disobeyed. "Sit perfectly still and hold on to Willie."

Irene and I, sauntering down Sherman street, saw them coming and took refuge in the treasurer's office, the nearest harbor at hand and the best place from which to view proceedings. They came up the street like a menagerie bereft of all the young of its varied species. The jailer attracted by all the turmoil was on the sidewalk to receive the children and turn them over to his wife behind locks and bars. The clang of the doors was not a moment too soon. With some difficulty and the assistance of the jailer, the sheriff and his worn-out deputy got the woman up the outside stairs of the courthouse to the office of the probate judge. I felt sorry for Father but I didn't see that I could be of any service to him. He probably would send me home if he saw me, so I allowed Irene to persuade me to continue our homeward way.

Halfway down the block we met old Mrs. Hayes, her drab-gray hair hanging around her face, the shabby old hat she rarely wore all awry, and her dingy skirt dragging in the dust. It was the only time I ever saw her when she did not want to stop and talk to me. She merely paused.

"That woman's a big fool," she said. "I gotta go see if I can do anything with her. Them men can't. Ain't she awful. She won't take any care of her children and she won't let anybody else."

Father decided in that hectic half hour in his office to send Julia and Willie to the Children's Home. Even he could see no aura of motherhood about the frowsy head of that wild woman.

213

Old Deadwood Days

That night Mrs. Hanson came back up to the jail. The jailer saw her coming into the yard and went to meet her prepared to lock her up if she persisted with her own peculiar methods in trying to see her children. She came directly toward him and almost threw a small bundle into his arms. It squirmed and wriggled a little and he tightened his hold protectingly.

"There," said the woman defiantly, "tell the the sheriff if he wants my family he can have 'em all. There's the baby." And she was gone.

The children were sent to the Children's Home and we heard gratifying accounts of them later on—of the way they grew up creditably in good homes. Mrs. Hayes missed them—even out of her sizable flock of black lambs that seemed never to diminish. As fast as one or two were taken away to better environments, others toddled in to take their places. She said: "They were good children—Julia and Willie, and they were smart."

When Calamity Jane Came Home

Chapter 8

WHEN CALAMITY JANE CAME HOME

ALAMITY JANE came back to Deadwood after her name had become a tradition. She was a glowing figure in the history of that hectic year of '76 that brought the gold rush into Deadwood Gulch, the crowds of men and scattering of women who followed high adventure wherever it led, and the glittering hopes and quick, easily forgotten tragedies of a town more than two hundred miles away by itself.

What Deadwood was in '76, a prosperous carefree outlaw town, colors its reputation even yet, and in the tense story of gold and guns, of lawless living and moral standards made for the moment, Calamity Jane was the one woman whose name has persisted with that of Wild Bill who was shot in a saloon in Deadwood that summer by Jack McCall, and of "Preacher Smith," the quiet kindly clergyman who was killed by Indians one Sunday morning in August as he walked alone out of Deadwood with his Bible under his arm and in his pocket the sermon he meant to preach in Crook City nearly ten miles away.

It was Calamity Jane who voiced the pity of it when they brought him back to Deadwood on a load of hay that had been passing.

Old Deadwood Days

"Ain't it too bad," she said to her friend Kitty Arnold as they prepared him for burial, "that the Indians killed the only man that came into the Hills to tell us how to live. And we sure need the telling."

She came back to Deadwood as quietly as she had slipped out, unheralded, dressed in shabby clothes, and leading her little seven-year-old girl by the hand. She was Mrs. Burke then and was considering the schooling of her daughter. Scores of women who looked like her came and went on Deadwood's streets unnoticed every day. But no one like Calamity Jane ever had come into Deadwood Gulch. She not only was typical of old Deadwood. She was old Deadwood.

In the years she had been away the roaring young placer gold camp had grown into a small city—the distributing point for gold that was pounded out of quartz or melted out of refractory ores. The Black Hills no longer was a poor man's fortune field. Red Creek that ran heavy now with the dark vermilion tailings from the Homestake and Father DeSmet mines, had been a clear sparkling stream then glittering with placer gold. The pines had been thicker on the mountains that walled in the gulch, and the houses fewer. A negligible number of log cabins sat around on the lower hillsides then, and one-story buildings with false fronts crowded into the gulch to make a Main street. The long bull-teams still came into town with as much profanity and cracking of whips by the bull-whackers as in the old days but the street was macadamized and they didn't get stuck in the mud. A few three-story

When Calamity Jane Came Home

buildings had gone up on Main street, their highest windows looking up with a startled surprise as though they expected the moon would fall in some night, or at least a pine tree from the top of McGovern Hill. Homes had multiplied on Forest Hill along one side of each terraced street, and in Ingleside cuddled in the hollow where the gulch widened away from Sherman street and sloped gradually up to White Rocks and the ridge to the southeast. There was a brick schoolhouse at the upper end of Main street just before it left town and became the road to Central City. Down that road and past the schoolhouse, I remember, there used to come funeral processions on their way to Mount Moriah, the cemetery on the hill, when a miner had been killed in the up-gulch mines and, with a dramatic fitness that impressed us all as we stood on the schoolhouse steps and watched and listened, the brass band always played, "Flee as a Bird to the Mountain." The lilt of the melody and the high waiting mountain with its crooning pines seemed to take away all the sting of death. There were more churches than there had been in Calamity's day, and more children on the streets. A generation was growing up that knew Calamity Jane only as a colorful bit of local history.

Most of her old friends and comrades were gone. Wild Bill who, according to Calamity herself, was the only man she ever had loved, lay under a life-size pink stone statue of himself in Mount Moriah. The statue was more or less mutilated because the soft rosy sandstone offered a temptation to sight-seeing vandals with little knives. A wire screen had been strung around it as a protection but not until after a piece of Bill's nose and a number of chips from his coat and his long hair had been sacrificed to the vandalism that some people call souvenir collecting.

I was walking down Main street dawdling along as much as possible on an errand for my mother hoping something interesting would happen, when Father overtook me. He said my uncle the General, was looking for me. He wanted to introduce me to Calamity Jane. They were up on the corner opposite the bank now. Father's tone implied that he saw no real reason for my knowing Calamity Jane but didn't feel strongly enough on the subject to oppose it. I was glad Mother wouldn't know about it until it was too late to object. I turned and went in hot haste toward Lee street. Here was the venture that had been casting its purple shadow ahead into my subconscious mind and kept me from hurrying back to Forest Hill and my mother. If I had been summoned to meet Joan of Arc or Alice in Wonderland or the Ice King's Daughter, it would not have been more marvelous and unreal.

The General saw me coming and untangled himself from a crowd of men to come and meet me. A passage was opened for us and the General made the presentation ceremoniously. "Miss Jane," he said, "this is my niece, Estelline Bennett." She held out her hand and said she was pleased to meet me.

Once long before I had seen Calamity Jane. Maude Dennee and I met her on the street and she asked us if we didn't want some candy. Maude knew who she was and had told me when we saw her coming. We were afraid to go with her but we

When Calamity Jane Came Home

were more afraid to refuse so we went along, shaking in our shoes, into Goldberg's grocery where she tossed a silver dollar nonchalantly on the counter and said: "Give these little girls some candy." When Mr. Goldberg had given us each a large quantity of mixed candy and we had thanked her politely, she walked away, and I never saw her again until the General presented me at her court on the corner.

She was a plain woman, looking older probably than she really was. She wore a shabby dark cloth coat that never had been good, a cheap little hat, a faded frayed skirt, and arctic overshoes although the sidewalks were perfectly clear of snow and even the crossings were not muddy. It was late in the fall but it hadn't snowed since the last chinook. Calamity Jane had been only a name to me as she was to all my generation but the name had stood for a picturesque bit of adventurous romance that the woman who stood on the corner in front of Pat's Place didn't match at all. But even before I had time to be disappointed I sensed something about her that had assembled this group of the best pioneers to welcome her back to Deadwood. It was the most representative that the town could have assembled. Many among them were pioneers of '76 who in some way or other had known Calamity Jane in those early days. A few of them had come in a year or two later always regretting that their youth or some other trivial but insurmountable obstacle had held them back from that first dynamic rush into a life that never could be repeated, not even at Nome where they rushed by water, nor the Nevada gold fields

Old Deadwood Days

where prospectors went to gold stampedes in automobiles, just as they might have gone to the governor's reception or a mine-owner's wedding. A gold stampede in an automobile! If any little pack pony ever heard about that! These men were trying as I was to make up for what they had lost, by cultivating people like Calamity Jane whenever they could.

The General belonged to '76 and he had known Calamity Jane as he had known Wild Bill and Preacher Smith and a score of lesser notables. She was an old friend out of a gorgeous old life. Seth Bullock, too, was a '76 pioneer and had known Calamity as a matter of course. He had been the first sheriff in Deadwood, coming there from Montana where he had been prominent in the territorial legislature and on the *vigilante* committee. There were no finer Westerners of three distinct types than he, my father, and the General.

Other pioneers of the 'seventies whom I remember in that group gathered around Calamity Jane to give her welcome, were Porter Warner, the genial gray-haired editor of the *Times;* Bill Bonham of the *Pioneer,* the first daily paper in the Hills; Mike Russell, friend and hunting companion of Buffalo Bill; Dr. Babcock, who as far as I know was the first physician in Deadwood Gulch, Captain Gardner, and George Ayers. They were Deadwood's most esteemed citizens. I remember noticing at the time how few there were among them of what the papers called the "denizens of the badlands." And every one of them was remembering those days in '78 when Calamity Jane alone took care of the small-

When Calamity Jane Came Home

pox patients in a crude log cabin pest house up in Spruce Gulch around behind White Rocks, the tall limestone peak over which the belated morning sun shines down on Deadwood Gulch. Smallpox was the most dreaded scourge of the frontier towns. Usually people died because of dearth of nursing, of facilities for taking care of the sick, and bad sanitary conditions. For the same reasons, it spread with terrifying speed. Those who recovered came from their sick beds with marred faces. All that a town like Deadwood in '78 knew to do for smallpox patients was to set aside an isolated cabin and notify the doctor.

There were half a dozen patients in the small log pest house in Spruce Gulch when Doctor Babcock made his first visit. He said they were all very sick and he was going back after supper. No one offered to go with him, but when he went back he found Calamity Jane there.

"What are you doing here?" he asked.

"Somebody's got to take care of 'em," she replied. "They can't even get 'emselves a drink of water when they want it. You tell me what to do, Doc, and I'll stay right here and do it."

"You'll probably get the smallpox," he warned her.

"Yes I know. I'll have to take that chance. I can't leave 'em here to die all alone. Won't they have a better chance if I stay and do what you tell me?"

There was no question but what they would and he told her so. But he looked at her clear olive skin and the firm contours of her face and chin and reminded her that it was not only disease and death she risked. With women of Calamity Jane's sort, beauty was as important almost as life itself. It was their stock in trade. Beauty and bravery were Calamity Jane's best assets. It was doubtful if she ever would lose her courage but, without her beauty, what would she do with her life? He reminded her of this too. But she took nothing into account except that half a dozen very sick men needed her services desperately, and she stayed. The charmed life that had persisted through Indian arrows and guns, through desperate gun fights, various hazards and hardships, held her dark striking beauty for further destruction. She came unscathed through the long smallpox siege and most of her patients lived. Dr. Babcock believed that without her care not one of them could have pulled through.

She never left the pest cabin during those hard weeks except to make hurried trips down to Deadwood for supplies that the grocers gave her.

Calamity Jane, I have heard from outsiders, was a woman of many faults. She shattered the commandment that women are supposed to guard against the lightest crack, all the breakage of the third was at her tongue's end, and she was given to strong drink. This is the full category of her vices. I never heard anything about them from the people who had known her. Old Black Hillers seemed never to remember her faults. Certainly they attached no importance to them.

Mrs. Joe King had come into the Hills once in the same outfit with Calamity Jane. She knew her pretty well. One day, considerably later, Calamity

When Calamity Jane Came Home

came into Wertheimer's where Mrs. King and Mrs. Lardner were shopping and spoke to Mrs. King who returned the greeting cordially. "I used to know you," Calamity said, "when your hair was brown instead of gray the way it is now."

"Yes," Mrs. King acknowledged the old acquaintance.

"Will you let me have a quarter?"

"Are you hungry, Jane? If you are, I'll go with you into Frasiers and see that you get all you want to eat, and what you want. But if it's drink you want, you can't get it from me."

Calamity smiled, showing her white even teeth. "I'm not hungry," she laughed. "It's a drink I want. I see I'll have to go some place else." She went out as pleasantly as though she had a new case of rye under her arm.

More than anyone else who lived into the twentieth century, Calamity Jane was symbolic of old Deadwood. Her virtues were of the endearing sort. Her vices were the wide-open sins of a wide-open country—the sort that never carried a hurt. Some one said of her once that she was a contradiction of "The evil men do lives after them. The good is oft interred with their bones." Whatever there was of evil in Calamity's life has been long since forgotten. It is not living as anyone's haunting sorrow. The good she did will be on men's tongues until the last of the old stagecoach aristocracy is gone. It is not lost in the dust of the grave beside Wild Bill's.

They were glad glorious days that Calamity Jane brought back to Deadwood in the late 'eighties and flung about on the corner in front of Pat's Place until

Old Deadwood Days

the neat brick Syndicate building across the street
faded out of the picture and even I could remember
the low frame saloon that used to stand there with its
swinging doors hung on the bias and its suggestion
of cool mystery inside. I always wanted to go into
a saloon just once to see what was there. The tanta-
lizing glimpses, as the half doors swayed open and
shut, of sawdust on the floor and a line of men at
the bar with their feet on a rail, and a bartender in
a white apron eternally wiping off the bar, did not
account for their amazing popularity. I always had
a feeling that there must be more to it than that.
The prim, smug cement sidewalks too, dropped out
of sight and in their place board walks with holes
and a step every now and then stumbled along under
our eyes. And surely over there in front of the other
bank, there used to be a pine tree. Everything was
young and expectant and joyous. In the stories those
old-timers were telling, Deadwood of '76 had been
an excited little scrap of Heaven. That is—until
Calamity asked about Bummer Dan. She wanted to
know what had become of him. It was Bill Remer
who told her.

Slippery Sam—Did she remember Slippery Sam?
Yes, she did but she wished she didn't. He was sort
of a mess in anybody's memory.

Well, Slippery Sam had gone into the Bella
Union bar one night looking for trouble. He had
no particular grievance against the Bella Union, nor
against Sam Young, the bartender. His quarrel
was with life. All his mining claims were pockets
and he was unlucky at faro. He leaned against the
bar, a striking figure in his gaudy plaid overcoat.

When Calamity Jane Came Home

They all remembered Slippery's gorgeous plaid overcoat. The General said it always reminded him of Joseph's. Bed Rock Tom asked, "Joseph who?" He'd never known anybody named Joseph, or named anything else for that matter, who had any coat anything like Slippery Sam's. Colonel Thornby said it made a rainbow look like an old pair of overalls. Sam's coat and his old white Stetson pulled down over his eyes identified him anywhere—even across a score of changeful years. He threw his little sack of dust down on the bar. There was something offensive in the way he did it; something more offensive in the way he asked for a drink. When he expressed his opinion of the quality of the whisky served, and of the manner of man who served it, the bartender's patience was exhausted. He reached under the bar and delivered his ultimatum along the sight of his gun.

"If you show yourself around here again to-night, Slippery," he said, "I'll fill you so full of holes you won't hold baled hay."

Slippery went out without any remarks. Which in itself was more or less menacing. But nobody paid any attention to him. Down the street a little way, after he had stumbled over several irregularities in the sidewalk and narrowly escaped splashing his splendor in the mud, he met Bummer Dan on his way up to the Bella Union. Bummer Dan smiled pleasantly at Slippery Sam as they stopped a moment in the yellow lamp light from the windows of the Melodeon. He shivered a little and thrust his hands deeper into the pockets of his thin worn coat. Slippery Sam looked at his turned-up collar and noted the shiver. It was a still cold night somewhere below zero.

"Say, Dan," Slippery said with an unwonted genialness that would have warned anyone of a less trusting nature than Bummer Dan, "I'm just going down to get a buffalo coat Cold Deck Johnny's going to let me have while he's laid up, and I won't need this coat. You take it and wear it. You look cold."

"Sure you won't need it?"

"Sure. Can't wear two coats at once, can I? And we may get a chinook before Johnny gets out again."

Dan slipped into the coat and Sam turned into the Melodeon where it was warm and light and gay. He never had liked Bummer Dan anyhow. He hated a fellow that kept on grinning when he was down on his luck and cold.

Bummer Dan continued on his way to the Bella Union. When his gaudy overcoat appeared in the doorway, Sam, the bartender, pulled his gun and fired with true and fatal aim. An impromptu court met the next day to try Sam for murder and this was the verdict: "Inasmuch as the defendant did not kill the man he set out to kill, and did not mean to kill the man he did kill, we the undersigned find him not guilty."

And that was what became of Bummer Dan. Slippery Sam? Well you couldn't try a man for murder just because he lent his coat to a shivering friend on a cold night, could you?

Calamity forgot about her little girl and me when she muttered what she thought of Slippery Sam. Had they let him stay in Deadwood? She was as-

When Calamity Jane Came Home

sured that they had not. He had left town the next day wearing Cold Deck Johnny's buffalo coat, and no one had heard of him since. Calamity hoped the only thing she would ever hear about him would be that he was hanged.

When the welcoming group broke up and scattered, we walked away together, Calamity, the General, the little girl, and I. When some one called the General into his office on Lee street, we stayed outside and leaned against the iron railing that protected the stairway leading down to Julius's. And she told me, as one woman to another, about her ar'tics, and about why she had come back to Deadwood now.

"I gotta keep my ar'tics on," she explained, "because I gave my shoes to a woman comin' up on the train to Rapid City this morning. Hers was so worn out they didn't cover her feet, and anyhow I was comin' on up in the stage and you know that's comfortable and she was riding out forty miles to a ranch in an open wagon. They might get caught in a snow storm."

I attempted feebly to express my admiration for her kindliness but she paid no attention to me. Probably she thought I was very stupid. She talked about something else.

"I want to put her in a convent," she said, indicating the child who stood beside us, pleasant but quiet. "I'd like her to get some schooling. But I couldn't do it without I had some help, so I come back to Deadwood." She didn't say she knew she could count on her Deadwood friends. She just assumed that anybody knew that about Deadwood. "They're giving a benefit for me at the Green Front to-morrow night."

The Green Front was the tailings of the badlands. It had been caught on its way up-gulch after every bright streak and color had been left behind. It had no band ballyhooing in the street outside as the Gem Theater had. It had no drama, no curtained corners, and no faint hint of mystery. One didn't need to see beyond the square, bilious exterior to know how crude it was and how obvious. Tragically dramatic things never happened there as they did at the Gem—happenings growing out of a misunderstanding of its character. No one ever stumbled into the Green Front under the misapprehension of having found a place of glittering amusement. It was just bald and bad and ugly and it made no pretense of being anything else. The opening of its doors for Calamity Jane's benefit was the best thing it ever did and that in itself was a ribald riot.

Once there was some kind of a political meeting there with the usual crowd and entertainment, such as it was, cleared out for the first half of the night. Father had to go to that meeting—he always had to go to political meetings—and the rest of the family being away and he not wanting to leave me alone, took me with him. I went with some curiosity, but I found the interior just as dull and graceless as the outside. I had been to political meetings with my father in respectable places that looked very much the same. Loose drab wooden chairs had pulled themselves up into stiff, straight rows for the occasion looking like dignified drunken men. The

When Calamity Jane Came Home

smoky kerosene lamps did their best to veil the walls in obscurity but without much success. Not being cold enough for a fire, the huge ungainly iron heating stove, rusty and dirty, stood out brazenly as a thing made for heating, not for ornamentation.

"Why don't they have a fireplace instead?" I asked Father as we sat looking around while the crowd assembled. "It would look better."

"They're too expensive," he said, "both to build and to maintain."

"The Green Front's got more money than we have," I argued from a surety based on all I'd heard. "And we have a fireplace."

"We're interested in hearthsides," he said gently, "and the Green Front is not."

The only really distinctive bits about the place were the bar and a sign on the wall reading: "Gentlemen will not spit on the floor. Others must not."

I was visualizing the place as Calamity and I leaned against the iron railing and talked about her benefit.

"Everybody's buying tickets," she said. "I guess there won't be any trouble about getting her into St. Martin's." She spoke a little wistfully with a half question and against the grim picture of the Green Front I saw the pretty gray walls and gabled roof of the convent on the little hill above Sturgis in the foothills a little more than a dozen miles away. I could see the sweet, serene faces of the Swiss nuns walking with the children among the trees and flowers of their secluded grounds, and my eyes came back to the reality of Calamity Jane's face with its written story of more than forty years of hard, careless living.

I agreed with her that probably there wouldn't be any difficulty in getting the child in. I didn't know anything at all about it. Mac, the Saddler, came along and interrupted us just then, and while he was telling Calamity that she didn't look a day older than she did thirteen or fourteen years before, the General came out and said he thought we would better go home to dinner. The adieux he made to Calamity differed in no way from those he would have offered to the President's wife.

"You should have seen her at her best," he said a trifle mournfully as we climbed the three flights of the Lee street stairs to Williams street. "She doesn't belong in the kind of clothes she's wearing. She doesn't belong in this day and age. You should have known her when she wore fringed buckskin breeches and carried a gun. She is afraid of nothing, Indians or smallpox, or road agents. That sort of courage hasn't much chance now, with the Indians all herded up in the reservations, and smallpox patients in hospitals, and the road agents either reformed or in the penitentiary. There never was a gunman quicker on the trigger, nor a good Samaritan quicker to help the fellow that needed it. Not much chance nowadays to show those rough rugged virtues that made Calamity beloved."

The General was a little sad about these soft days that had come upon us, but if she wanted to put her daughter in the convent, he hoped she would get the money to do it. It was the nearest she ever had come to asking anything for herself. She didn't want to

When Calamity Jane Came Home

pass on exactly the sort of life she had lived and she knew a lot of people in Deadwood that she was sure would agree with her on that. She knew better than anyone else where she had made her mistakes and she didn't rate her virtues as highly as her friends did.

Our dinner-table talk that night was an expurgated edition of the life of Calamity Jane as the General and Father had known her and known about her from other pioneers of Deadwood. She came into the Black Hills first with General Crook's command in the summer of '75 when he had marched in from Fort Laramie to order the miners out of the Hills until treaties could be made with the Indians. Calamity had been in Cheyenne getting a little bored and restless when she heard of the proposed expedition into a new, wild, and dangerous country. The day she heard about it, she hired a team and buggy to "go for a little ride," she told the man at the livery stable. She drove her horses at an easy trot through the streets of Cheyenne, but when she had left the city behind she speeded up and drove as rapidly as her consideration for horses would permit. Arrived at Fort Laramie, she left her rig where its owner could recover it, smuggled herself in among the soldiers, and was too far on the way to the outlaw country to be sent back, before anyone discovered she was a woman.

The General had known her first when she came in with Wild Bill, Colorado Charley, and some others in '76. He was one of those who was entirely blind to her faults and very kind to her virtues. Father's acquaintance with her had been slight. She was the sort of woman who did not interest him in any way and he was indifferently willing to accept the General's estimate of her.

Martha Jane Canary, the General said, rolling the name around behind his blond mustache and beard, was a person of so little consequence that no one knew with any exactness where she was born or from what sort of people she came. By the time she got to be Calamity Jane notorious from the Missouri river to the heart of the Rockies, and from Denver to old Fort Benton, she herself didn't seem to be quite sure. According to one story, she was born near Burlington, Iowa, about the year 1851, the daughter of a Baptist clergyman, and had run away when she was very young, with an army lieutenant and gone to Wyoming. At Sidney, Nebraska, she gave birth to a son and the young officer who was its father had sent it back to his parents in "the States," telling them a romantic tale about finding the waif on the plains after its parents had been killed by Indians.

A less interesting account gave Calamity's birthplace as Princeton, Missouri, fixing the date definitely as May 1, 1852. It made no mention of her family, but did tell of the seductive young lieutenant, and sent the baby to an orphan asylum.

The General was inclined to believe what an old bull-whacker had told him. The bull-whacker had known Jane when she was a little girl in Fort Laramie and he said she was born at La Bonte's trading post one hundred and twenty miles northwest of Fort Laramie in 1860, and when she was only two years old her father had been killed and her mother seriously wounded by Sioux Indians. Some one brought her down to Fort Laramie where she was

When Calamity Jane Came Home

adopted by an army sergeant and his wife. "They were awful kind to her," the bull-whacker had told the General, "but they didn't learn her nothing, and she just run wild around the post."

It was after the affair with the lieutenant that Calamity's mother came into the picture again and Calamity Jane went with her and her stepfather, a man by the name of Hart, to Salt Lake City, where she stayed peaceably for a very brief period. Then she ran away again. This time she went to Rawlins, Wyoming, where she led a wild life according to all reports except those given to her stepfather when he came after her. He was convinced from all he saw and heard that she had developed into a hard-working, well-behaved young woman, and he went back to Utah and let her stay.

Some one from Montana told me once that Jane came honestly by her *penchant* for sinning because her mother was the famous Madame Canary of the Montana mining camps. Her houses were considered "high class" and possibly she would not have wanted her wild, out-door young daughter with her even if she had cared to come, which probably she would not.

Calamity Jane drifted restlessly about through the frontier camps and army posts of Wyoming, Nebraska, and Montana learning to tie a diamond hitch with deft fingers, to pack horses, and handle teams with firm, gentle expertness. For a while she held a government position with a pack train. She was willing to do any sort of work that could be done out of doors, or inside when there was sickness and need of nursing, and she cast her lot lightly with any man

Old Deadwood Days

who lived and worked out of doors and who followed new trails.

In another age and in different surroundings, she might have been a famous horsewoman or athlete. If she had lived in the days of the Great War, she would have worn a Red Cross uniform at the front where the danger was greatest and the need of the wounded most urgent.

Living in a time that kept its women by the hearthstone, in the back seat of a carriage, and in the side-saddle, she found little legitimate outlet for her tremendous vital energy and her dominant love of excitement. And so she went her way along the frontier, with freighters, soldiers, and placer miners, helping blaze the way and holding out a strong hand to the weaker brothers across the hard places, until her crooked trail led her in the middle 'seventies to Deadwood where she seemed to find a home foothold she never had known before. It was the place to which she kept coming back as she got older. It was with Deadwood, her name was most closely associated, although all the Black Hills knew her.

Father remembered having seen her once in Rapid City coming out of an old log hotel.

"Say, Judge," she said, addressing Father because he was the only person within easy reach of her voice, "I wonder if I hadn't ought to've done it. Maybe I hadn't. I took that sick kid in there some pickles because he wanted them so bad and the doctor wouldn't let him have 'em. He said he'd die if he ate 'em and the kid thought he'd die if he didn't. He's got mountain fever."

She looked at Father for a moment, not worried

When Calamity Jane Came Home

but thoughtful. He had nothing to advise. The thing was done and he didn't know much about taking care of mountain fever patients anyway. He would have left it to the doctor but there was no use in saying that now.

"Well," she said finally in a matter-of-fact tone, "I guess it's up to me to see that he don't die." And she did.

The incident had been recalled to Father only the week before in Custer. He had happened to meet "the kid," in town from his prospect up in the mountains, to get supplies. He told Father then that he owed his life to Calamity Jane's nursing. Perhaps to the pickles, too. You never could tell.

The telephone interrupted just then and the General who sat with his back to it, answered and summoned Mother. Her one-sided conversation showed a good deal of vexation. It was Mrs. Van Cise, she said when she sat down, and she said she had just had word from two different women that they wouldn't let their young daughters dance in the kirmiss they were going to give for the church if that little girl whose mother was out here to get a divorce wasn't taken out. They said they understood the child's father was in the penitentiary although the mother was getting a divorce on the grounds of desertion.

Father interrupted to say that the woman was his client and a very fine woman and her husband was not in the penitentiary, although he ought to be on general principles. He was just a good-for-nothing hoodlum that wouldn't support his family.

"Well," Mother said, "they say too that there is

something queer about that man that's always around with her, and anyway she is too popular with the men to be all right. Mrs. Van Cise doesn't know what to do and neither do I. That child is the best dancer we have. They say she dances too well to be a lady's child."

"I thought they were giving this for the church," the General commented. "How about the publicans and sinners? Aren't they even permitted to help raise money to pay the preacher? Are they allowed to come to church?"

Mother was willing about that time to have the conversation come back to Calamity Jane.

The General told about the one time she had been arrested in Deadwood. Father remembered hearing about it and the General told it to Mother who would not have encouraged him before her telephone conversation.

A man got drunk in a resort and when he sobered up a little found his roll of thirty dollars was gone. He had two or three girls in the place arrested, including Jane, and they all appeared before Justice Hall. Without any questioning or parley, Calamity Jane admitted that she had taken the thirty dollars away from him when he was dead drunk.

"If I hadn't," she said, "some of the other girls would."

The justice asked what she had done with it and she said she had paid the hospital bills of one of the girls who was sick, very sick, and broke.

Calamity was set free and the denunciation of the court was turned on the plaintiff. If he would stay sober and out of disreputable houses he wouldn't

When Calamity Jane Came Home

have to pay other people's hospital bills. In this case, the disposition of the money stood.

From where I sat at Father's right, I could see the red-berried rowan tree that Father had bought somewhere and planted in the small rectangle made by the ell of the dining room. It always made me think of a story I had read once about a Scotch clergyman who, when life's perplexities weighed heavily on him, went out and sat down under his rowan tree and it nodded its green leaves and scarlet berries wisely at him and said: "Dinna' fash yoursel', MacQuatrie, the Lord God Almighty is a reasonable body." Of course He is, I thought to myself, reasonable enough to expect people, even women, to take note of the fact that He went to considerable trouble to make nine other Commandments besides the seventh.

"Do you remember, Judge," the General was saying when I brought my attention back to the table, "the time Calamity pulled a gun and a volley of language on a bull-whacker down here because he was belaboring a tired ox? He didn't dare even frown at the beast when she got through with him."

I could see beyond the rowan tree now, through the narrow gap of Wall street to Main. It was beginning to get dark and the lamps were lighted in the corner buildings that faced me. Slowly dragging past came a late bull train. It came only from Rapid City now but the last ten miles were up a steep hard grade through the mountains. I saw a bull-whacker flourish his long whip that filled the narrow opening like a slim twisting smoke spiral. He didn't seem to be abusing his oxen. They were going right along, slowly, but patiently and steadily. I wondered whether, if he did get brutal, there was any woman in Deadwood now who would stop him.

The General was just well launched in a story about Calamity and Antelope Frank fighting Indians from the precarious shelter of a buffalo wallow after their horses had been shot from under them, when the doorbell rang and we all went into the front parlor in a bunch to visit with Mrs. McLaughlin whose husband was a friend of Father's, one of the best lawyers at the bar, and the first mayor of Deadwood. She said Calamity Jane probably was the only woman in the world who ever ran away from her husband because he gave her too many good clothes and too soft living. That was her second husband. His name was White and he had sold some mining property for quite a lot of money not long after he married Calamity Jane. Mrs. McLaughlin said she used to see Calamity occasionally on the street in Cheyenne and she was a pretty girl then, slim, dark eyed, and dark haired, and when White made money the first thing he thought of was to deck her out in fine clothes. He had to buy them because she wasn't enough interested, and she found them uncomfortable and cumbersome. They lived about at the best hotels in Cheyenne and Denver, and she didn't feel at home. She stood the clothes and the hotels as long as she could, and then she ran away. She was with a freighting outfit dressed like a man when he found her and was convinced of the futility of trying to get her back. He never did.

The way Calamity's benefit worked out showed

exactly why she had stumbled so much through life. She didn't have the caliber to carry through her own best plans. She couldn't always "build above the deep intent, the deed."

The benefit at the Green Front was a howling success—just that. I don't know how many people went, but I understand there were plenty, and a great many more bought tickets. The money poured in—gold and greenbacks, as lavishly as though it had been gold dust and the time, 1876. There was enough to have kept that child in St. Martin's convent until she was ready for Wellesley or Bryn Mawr. The Green Front turned it over to Calamity and she walked up to the bar to treat the crowd for having been so kind to her child. Her friends tried, after the first drink, to curb her lavishness, but she forgot all about the young daughter, the convent, and higher education for women, and got roaring drunk.

I heard her myself in the early dark of the morning. She was going up and down Main street and she woke me out of a sound slumber in my little bed on Forest Hill. Ordinary revelry would not have disturbed me in the least, but rarely did an individual make so much and such continuous noise. Usually it took a crowd to create so wild a disturbance. Calamity's voice was loud and it had a carrying quality. I recognized it easily as I listened.

Most people would have been stopped in their high revelry somewhere toward morning, but it never would have occurred to Deadwood's night policeman, nor to anyone else in authority to question Calamity Jane's pleasures, even though they woke the entire town. She herself would not have disturbed the sleep of an alley kitten if she had known. If she thought about it at all in her hilarious mind that night, she probably supposed nobody else had gone to bed yet. When she had known the town it was not Deadwood's custom to sleep at night.

I know she was specially privileged because other people did get run in for drinking too loud. And the way I know is that once when Father was city attorney he always gave all the drunk and disorderly fees to Mother and the way she used to peruse the morning paper to see how many drunk and disorderlies there had been was a never failing amazement to the family. Gaylord, my young brother, said she seemed to want the population to "go out with the boys and get drunk and then holler," and his personal acquaintance with her had led him to believe quite the contrary.

Some of Calamity's friends rescued her purse before all the money was gone, but she took her child and left town the next day.

It was a long time before Calamity Jane came back to Deadwood again. When she did she was alone. I understand her daughter did get an education, and grew up and married well, but it was far away from the temptations of Deadwood and Calamity's old friends.

Her last coming was early in the twentieth century —an anachronism, a bit of an alien even in her old haunts. She was a broken, sick woman, worn out at fifty with the hard careless life she had led. She

When Calamity Jane Came Home

went merrily through a few more gay carousals and then, on the second of August, the twenty-seventh anniversary of the murder of Wild Bill, she died in a miners' boarding house in the gold camp of Terry up in the mountains above Deadwood. It was a high, wild mining camp, perhaps reminding Calamity more of old Deadwood than did Deadwood itself.

She was buried from the Methodist Church in Deadwood. The sermon was preached by Dr. C. B. Clark, one of the most eminent clergymen ever in the Hills, who, his son Badger Clark, says: "In his long life has seldom been conscious of a man's rough exterior, or unconscious of his obscurest virtue." It was a sermon that took no account of the irregularities of her conduct but stressed her high virtues. The church was crowded and a long line of carriages followed Calamity Jane to her grave beside Wild Bill.

The last people leaving the church noticed that a man in the front pew who had attracted their attention during the service by his grief, was still kneeling and sobbing bitterly. No one knew him, but some one went up and touched him on the shoulder and asked if he had known Calamity Jane.

"Yes," he said between sobs, "I was her first husband. She was the finest woman that ever lived—the kindest."

The Stagecoach Aristocracy

Chapter 9

THE STAGECOACH ARISTOCRACY

A N aristocracy is built on the oldest and most enduring phase of a country's civilization. It may trace its pride of race to the achievements of the white-plumed Henry of Navarre or to the conquests of William of Normandy, to the long hard voyage of the *Mayflower* or to the rumbling, stumbling journeys of the old Deadwood stagecoach. The childen of pioneers, who prove their own mettle inherit the power and the prestige. The years and the generations weed out the unfit.

Deadwood in the Black Hills, looking back to a tumultuous outlaw mining camp at the end of a long hazardous stagecoach trail, built its aristocracy after the fashion of every other country. It went back to the beginning, for as far as Deadwood was concerned the world was born in the spring of 1876. No man brought his past into Deadwood. Many left their right names back in the States. Their own personal histories, failures, and achievements counted for nothing at all in the new gold camp; those of their fathers and grandfathers, for far less.

It was Henry Keets, one of the finest of the old-time cattle men, who coined the phrase, "stagecoach aristocracy," and defined it after the era of its building was past.

Old Deadwood Days

"The railroads," he said, "have brought in a lot of fine people, good citizens that we're glad to have. But they're different. They don't belong to the stagecoach aristocracy. The foundations had all been laid and the framework was up when they arrived.

"Those who came in by stage had a certain flair of vision and a steadiness of purpose. They are the movers and shakers of the world. They are the aristocrats of the frontier."

The stagecoach aristocracy built itself up through the prospecting and placer gold days of Deadwood Gulch, through the years when you could see free gold in the pan and in the quartz, pan it out, pound it out, and catch it on quicksilver plates. No one in those days was mining refractory ore—the evasive, furtive member of the gold family that skulks in solution in the rocks. The General always insisted that there might be an older aristocracy than anything we knew. How about the prospectors who built the lost cabin over by Polo Creek? How about the Indians? And how about those fellows who evidently had abandoned their rich ore vein at Gold Run in a hard battle, or perhaps all been killed? There was plenty of evidence to prove that the proud pioneers of the 'seventies might have found only the tailings of a rich old gold field from which some earlier Argonauts had reaped a fabulously rich golden harvest. The thought appealed to the General's imagination. He liked to expand it.

The lost cabin was in his mind especially one night when we had a small dinner party quickly ar-

The Stagecoach Aristocracy

ranged that afternoon when he telephoned that Judge Romans had given him some pheasants. At the table he told us that Romans had been out hunting with old Mineral Jack in the neighborhood of the lost cabin and had brought back a full bag of pheasants. Bob Mulford, the new metallurgist at the Iron Hill, asked about the lost cabin.

It was a crude log cabin, the General said, standing in a cluster of pine and spruce trees over near Polo Creek, and was in a dilapidated, decayed condition when it was discovered early in '76 by some miners prospecting for gold. There was no door to the cabin and but one small window which would seem to indicate that the inhabitants lived in continual fear of the Indians. It was a very rude piece of workmanship, built of logs of uneven length which, when the cabin was discovered, had begun to decay. The roof was of pine boughs covered with dirt. A number of trees had been felled near the cabin and logs had been cut from them. In one of these was found a wooden wedge and not far from the cabin was an old location stake.

Mr. Remer said that Mineral Jack had been hunting that lost cabin mine for nearly ten years. He supposed he would go on hunting it as long as he lived. There was a fairly well defined trail leading away from the cabin but it got lost under some fallen trees and a little deer trail leading down to Polo creek.

It sounded to me like an Arabian Night's tale and I asked Robbie if he knew where it was. He said he didn't exactly but from what they said he thought he could find it, and we decided to make up

Old Deadwood Days

a searching party of two at the first opportunity, but somehow we never did.

The lost cabin was only one of many proofs of a long-forgotten gold rush. There was an abandoned mine up in Gold Run where work evidently had been stopped suddenly. It had a rich vein of ore in which a cut had been run years before the Deadwood Gulch stampede of '76. The timbers in the gulch showed marks of having stood for many years, and were full of bullet holes indicating a terrible siege. All through the Whitewood district great hewed pine logs had been found overgrown with pines long since past their youth. Shot and bullets had penetrated some of this timber.

Somewhere a wagon chain still dangled from a lofty pine, embedded by years of tree growth in the trunk. Mr. Remer had seen that once while riding horseback through the mountains and found, when he spoke of it, that it was pretty well known to old-timers. Dick Brown had told him that once in the late 'seventies while he and some other men were digging for a smokehouse in the rear of the Gem Theater they found, about eight feet below the surface, a pair of iron gads, bent and worn by service and perforated with rust holes. That reminded Father of the grindstone that was found by men excavating in the rear of Morton's saloon when they struck bedrock about six feet below the level surface. It was of native rock and looked to be in perfect condition but when it was exposed to the air it fell apart.

Sluice boxes had been found buried from six to seven feet under the earth, showing by their stages

250

of decay that they were from twenty to thirty years old when the first known white man washed gold in Deadwood Gulch. As late as May, '81, some prospectors working a claim in Deadwood Gulch found, about four feet below the surface, a rusty old pick with a handle of hardwood almost decayed away.

Ghosts seemed to sit around our candle-lit table— ghosts of long-forgotten gold prospectors. Arrowheads and bits of pottery dug up in countries known to have old histories are interesting enough. But to find in a perfectly new country—a country you thought had been discovered only the year before yesterday—tools that human hands had used in a bygone generation, following a craft you knew—that was like building a perfectly new pine-smelling frame shack and coming down from finishing the roof, to see King Solomon sitting in a musty old chair counting his four hundred and twenty talents from the golden wedge of Ophir.

Then there were the Indians. The General had known the Indians in '76 when they were behaving their worst, yet his strongest feeling about them was one of concern because of the way they had been robbed and abused. When Kung-Ke-Shunka (Crow Dog), a captain of police on the Rosebud reservation, was tried in Deadwood for the killing of Spotted Tail, a Rosebud chief, in 1881, the General was moved to rather modern metered verse in his behalf. It began:

> "Why of all my race in this my native land
> Am I the first to feel the heavy hand
> Of the ruthless invader?"

Old Deadwood Days

Spotted Tail was an unprincipled old Indian addicted to the habit of eloping with other men's wives, and so when Crow Dog killed him for what generally was conceded to be a perfectly justifiable reason, whatever it was, none of the Indians seemed to care very much. Crow Dog paid Spotted Tail's family eight horses, fifty dollars in money, and one blanket valued at forty dollars, and Spotted Tail's shade, his family, and justice, all were supposed to be satisfied.

Then, for the first time in the history of the red race, an Indian was arrested and brought to trial in the white man's court for a crime against another Indian. The United States court had been too busy straightening out the tangled troubles of the white men in the new country to bother about the internal affairs of the Sioux.

I sat behind my father in the court room during the Crow Dog trial and watched the expressionless face of the old defendant with a growing resentment in my heart against my own people. Why couldn't we let the Indians alone? There was no doubt, even in my young mind that Crow Dog had had ample provocation, and the world was better off without Spotted Tail. Even the prosecution did not make him either a worthy or a lovable citizen. Furthermore, it had been the unquestioned right of Indian braves since the beginning of time to settle their own affairs in their own way.

Crow Dog sat behind his lawyer, Mr. Plowman whom he called "The-Little-Man-with-the-Big-Voice," with never a flicker of expression on his fine, dignified old face. He was conscious of no

The Stagecoach Aristocracy

wrongdoing and he took things as they came. When they brought in a verdict of "guilty" I cried and my father sent me home. I felt much worse about it, apparently, than Crow Dog did. He calmly asked permission to go back to his home on the Rosebud reservation for the purpose of closing up his affairs. He wanted to observe the formality of distributing his ponies among the young men of his tribe, and say good-by to his family. He promised to come back to be hanged on the date set, and they let him go alone. Down at the agency the trader asked in very natural surprise if he were going back—back to be hanged. He answered in a matter-of-fact way that he had "promised the Little-Man-with-the-Big-Voice." The old-time Indians knew nothing about a broken promise. When they gave their word they kept it.

Crow Dog came back as he promised, but the Little-Man-with-the-Big-Voice had appealed to the United States Supreme Court and the old Indian who kept his word was acquitted.

The day of his release Crow Dog went around the courtroom and shook hands with everybody, but the Little-Man-with-the-Big-Voice who had saved him from ignominious death, he kissed. Then he went out of the court room with a yell, got into a wagon and drove off.

The stagecoach aristocracy as we knew it, made up neither of prehistoric prospectors nor Indians, had some trouble getting started. A woman came in and shot up the first perfectly nice dance given in Deadwood. Mr. Goldberg, the pioneer grocer, told Irene and me about it one day when we were buying candy for the Congregational Sunday School Christmas tree. Irene and I would have had a beautiful time sampling bonbons and chocolates if she hadn't been so conscientious and firm about tasting only the inexpensive varieties we had instructions to buy. So we munched striped candy and hard gum drops while Mr. Goldberg told us about that first ball.

He said everybody was young in '76 and wanted to have a good time. So a bunch of bachelors and married men who didn't care specially for the Melodeon and Bella Union brand of pleasure organized a sort of informal club to give dances during the winter in hotel dining rooms or empty new stores. There was no difficulty about music. Violinists and cornetists came in with the earliest of the gold seekers. Piano players preceded the first square piano hauled in by oxen.

The first of these parties, given in the I X L dining room, was historic because it was the first polite social affair given in Deadwood. That is, it started out politely. The invitation list had been carefully prepared and all the men who had wives brought them. Some brought their little daughters. There were no young ladies and there were hordes of men.

When the caller sang out his first: "Partners for a quadrille," there was no scent of battle smoke in the close little dancing hall.

"Salute your partners, and first and second couples forward and back." Waltzes and polkas and lanciers and more quadrilles followed and everything was going along merrily and mannerly. The caller had just shouted above the fiddles, the horns, and the drums: "Grand right and left," when a painted lady in a low-cut red satin gown pushed peremptorily past the man at the door, and lifted up her voice loudly and defiantly.

Her man was there and she was just as good as he was. If he could come to this "damn tony dance," she'd come too. She'd like to see anybody stop her. An impromptu floor committee closed around the unwelcome guest and told her what they thought of a lady who would come uninvited to a party. But she continued to voice her disapproval of the double standard, and finally to emphasize her opinion properly, she pulled her gun and proceeded to shoot things up. The women and children were hurried away. The infuriated man whom she had followed, finally got her gun away from her and persuaded her violently out of the place. Everybody left in confusion and the dance was over.

But the club was not discouraged. It merely took a little more precaution about its membership. It coudn't have gentlemen attached to women who wanted to go about shooting up nice parties. Of his own accord the man responsible for the disorder never came again and the club danced peaceably on through the winter.

That was the only blatant infringement of the social order on record in Deadwood. The stagecoach aristocracy had established itself unconsciously and drew the cordon closely as the years went on. It was an aristocracy that had nothing at all to do with riches. Le Baron E. de Maudat-Grancey, one of the many Frenchmen who had extensive interests in the Black Hills in the 'seventies and early 'eighties was astonished at the casual joking way in which Deadwood referred to its poverty. He thought about it a good deal and finally wrote home that: "In this country the man who to-day has nothing to eat will to-morrow in prospecting find a mine of fabulous riches. Poverty here is but transitory and not, as in Europe a habitual state, a sort of degradation."

The fiddler of Dooney had a far and wide following in Deadwood—the good people on the mountain side and the upper reaches of the gulch, and those who, "by an evil chance," were caught in the snares of the badlands. We loved the fiddle and we loved to dance.

We danced all the time on any excuse and no excuse. Balls were given for the benefit of churches, hospitals, volunteer fire departments, the Spearfish Academy that later was the State Normal School, and to celebrate the opening of new business houses. We all gave big dancing parties in our homes, especially those of us who had double parlors and perhaps a dining room or bedroom connecting with double doors. Our house was like that and others were the McPhersons, Hasties, Van Cises, Bullocks, Shotwells, and John R. Wilsons. I remember a reception Mrs. Shotwell gave one winter just after she had decorated her parlor with a frieze of scarlet and yellow autumn leaves just below the ceiling and she used kinnikinick and Oregon grape leaves everywhere. She had done it all herself, even the high frieze. It was lovely, and she asked Irene and me, who helped her, to dress the part and I wore a red dress and Irene a yellow one.

The Stagecoach Aristocracy

The Blackstones living at the De Smet mine about two miles up Deadwood Gulch, had a big rambling house with broad terraces and everything to make it a perfect setting for parties including the night drive that was just far enough in those days of horses, and the charming, hospitable Blackstones themselves. As hosts they always were in practice. Guests came and went continuously, in carriages, in hacks, on horseback, and on foot. They came up Deadwood Gulch, down Poorman, and through the long Homestake tunnel from Lead that led around the giant spicy woodpile of fragrant fresh-cut pine. It stood at the neutral crossroads of Deadwood and Lead society. Once I arrived at one of their big balls to find Louise and Flora, the Blackstone twins, in the dressing room upstairs struggling to make up to Mrs. John R. Wilson for the lack of a maid. She had on a stunning ivory velvet gown trimmed with crystals, and she had come bearing in a bag the adjustable court train that was fastened on the shoulders and under the arms in most intricate fashion, and trailed for at least a yard on the floor. Having nothing to do to my pink tulle but fluff it out, I went to the assistance of Louise and Flora whose eyes were dancing with admiration. In the course of considerable time while guests came in, powdered their noses and went down stairs, and the orchestra tuned its violins and played "The Beautiful Blue Danube," we followed the long impressive velvet train downstairs. Mrs. Wilson was a beauty and that night she was all a-sparkle with diamonds. Flora and Louise, who were just coming to the edge of their doll days, studied her very carefully with the idea of repeating her in their doll families as far as was humanly possible. I worked with them diligently over that miniature adjustable train the next week and wished I were young enough to play with dolls. I wished that just long enough to remember that when I played with dolls I never went to dancing parties—these gorgeous dancing parties for which the heavy furniture was all moved away somewhere else, canvas was spread over the carpets, elaborate suppers were served at midnight, and everybody stayed till morning.

In the gray of one cold winter dawn Father, Mother, and I, coming down Centennial avenue from a ball at the Wilsons met Alvin Clark delivering the *Pioneer*. Once on a summer morning the General and I came home from the Blackstones and when we reached our own front steps he suggested that we sit down and watch the sun rise.

"See how rosy it is over White Rocks? It won't be but a few minutes now. It's something you really ought to see once at least in your lifetime, and dear knows you'll never see it from the other end."

Mrs. McPherson's most famous ball was known afterwards much to her disgust as "Mrs. McPherson's Iron Hill party." She gave a great many dancing parties but this was the most elaborate of them all. It was in March but supper was served in a spacious tent on the terrace. The wide veranda that sprawled around two sides of the house was enclosed with canvas and we danced out from the parlors through the long French windows on to the porch and back again. The only flaw in the party

The Stagecoach Aristocracy

was the aftermath. Professor Hirschfeld told Mrs. McPherson that Mrs. Kingsley had said, "Iron Hill would tell," just as though Mrs. McPherson never had been able to give a party until the Iron Hill silver mine paid dividends. And Mrs. Kingsley told her that Mr. Remer had said, "Professor Hirschfeld made the deviled eggs for supper," just as though she couldn't make deviled eggs herself.

There never were as many as half a dozen girls at those parties and no one of us was of marriageable age. There were no young ladies, but there were millions of bachelors, young and middle-aged. That may have been one reason why the bachelors were so easily intrigued in ways we knew nothing about at the time.

A man I knew told me long years afterwards that when he first came out from the East and went to work in one of the banks, he read one morning in the paper that "Miss Mollie Johnson would give a masked ball Saturday night in California George's restaurant." It sounded so sociable to a young man in a strange camp and the invitation seemed to be so general that he naïvely spoke of it to Mr. Mund, cashier of the bank and superintendent of the Congregational Sunday School.

"I see a Miss Johnson is going to give a masked ball," he began, when Mr. Mund cut him short.

"Well, don't let me catch any of you boys going down to that dance. Anybody that goes will be fired."

That whetted the curiosity of the young man just out of the East and he asked the other young men in the bank about it. No one of them was fired. Mr. Mund would have had no way of "catching them at the dance," unless he went himself.

The first young ladies I remember in our own circle were two from the South who were visiting up at one of the mines. They were quite old. I think one was twenty-four. We were going out on flat cars over the Homestake wood road to Horseshoe Grove where a picnic was being given in their honor, when I heard Mrs. Kingsley say to her co-chaperon, Mrs. Tracy, that "our girls don't seem to have much chance against these Southern belles." She thought they were getting too much attention away from her young daughter, Lulu, and me. I thought so too now that my attention was called to it. Before that I had been absorbed in watching their methods. Mrs. Tracy said it was because they were experienced.

"Ours are very young," she comforted. "Give them a year or two."

Mose Lyon confirmed Mrs. Kingsley's fear. Never would he have taken the trouble for us that he did for them. He came over on horseback from the Buxton mine dressed just as he had come out of the shaft and danced with these pretty things in their flowered organdies as gayly and confidently as though he had just come from the hands of an English valet instead of the bottom of a muddy mine. Our light summer frocks had known his mine-messed flannel arms before. One never could tell what Mose would do. He liked contrast. He was immaculate in his evening clothes. And he liked to wear rough miners' togs, but it seemed to me he never had ap-

ONE OF THE STAIRS LEADING TO A TERRACED STREET

The Lee Street stairs from Main Street to Williams Street, the first terrace on Forest Hill. The little house at the head of the stairs on the right was where Preacher Smith lived in 1876.

(From an old photograph.)

The Stagecoach Aristocracy

peared anywhere before looking just like this. He wore high heavy boots covered with red mud from his underground workings. His corduroys and his flannel shirt were lost under the mud and thick candle drippings. We all expostulated with him. He had no right to go anywhere to dance looking like that. But he just laughed, the resonant ringing laugh for which he was famous.

He wasn't around when we danced our last dance and boarded the return train. He was off riding like a young Lochinvar through the mountains. When we pulled into the little station, there he was on the platform. We knew him, of course—we, his old friends, when we looked through the car window and saw him waiting, but the young ladies from the South had to be introduced all over again. He was a regular Mr. Cinderella with a fairy godfather up at his mine, and his horse's feet had been shod with lightning. He stood there like a model for the well-dressed man, in frock coat and patent leather pumps, his cane over his arm, and his high silk hat in his hand. He could not have been disappointed in the sensation he created.

We amused ourselves for the most part after the fashion of people in less remote communities. We danced at picnics, rode horseback, had porch parties, and played tennis in the summer, and in the winter we danced, played the piano and sang for each other because our opportunities for professional musical entertainment were rare, and gave dinner parties, and sleighing parties out to the Cliff House for supper.

Our dinner parties were second in favor only to

261

the dances. They gave us opportunity for conversation and we were a talky people. We set our tables conventionally with fine linen, cut glass, silver, china, candles, and flowers, and served game and buffalo berry or chokecherry jelly without realizing at all how rare were our menus. There was no closed season on game and deer hung in front of the markets more common than beef. We could have had buffalo steaks and bear roasts if we had wanted them but my mother and her friends scorned them. They would have preferred barnyard chickens to grouse, and a rib roast of beef to venison. Less than one hundred miles northwest of Deadwood in the 'eighties, buffalo ran in herds of ten thousand and, according to hunters who brought them in by the wagonload, they were "thicker than hair on a dog's back." Dried buffalo tongue was an available but unpopular luxury. Beside the game and wild fruits at our dinner parties we served "things that grow out West in cans."

And we talked. The older men reminisced and out of the days of the 'seventies dug up half-forgotten stories of adventure and mystery.

One night Mrs. Cheairs was giving a dinner in her high dining room that hung out over the hill in what strangers always thought a most perilous position. Far below in the gulch was one of the worst stretches of the badlands. The dance music, probably not so very good if we had been nearer, came up the steep hill very gay and friendly. It was early in the fall and through the windows came a delicious odor of far-off burning pine trees. The candles on the table wore festive rose-colored shades

The Stagecoach Aristocracy

and the prairie chicken had just been served when the sound of a shot sung out above the music in the gulch and the happy voices around the table. It cut Mose Lyon's famous laugh abruptly, and everyone rushed to the window. Down around the Blue Front that backed into the foot of the hill, we saw a crowd assembling. People were pushing and jostling, some to get in to the scene of trouble, and some to hurry away. But the music had stopped and everything was very quiet. With a lively instinct to be the first to tell something of importance, I slipped to the telephone and called the *Pioneer*.

"Hello, Mr. Bonham? Yes. Yes. Something's happened down here at the Blue Front. I think it's a murder. I thought you'd want to send somebody down."

"All right, I'll send Blondy right down. But, wait a minute, Estelline," in his soft, slow drawling voice. "How do you happen to be down at the Blue Front?"

All the excitement seemed to be over by that time. The crowd had gone inside or dispersed and we went back to our prairie chicken and memories of the days when shots were more common than now, and something reminded Father of a mysterious moonlight duel.

Colonel Thornby remembered it, too, and urged the telling of the story.

"It is an illustration of the trite saying that truth is stranger than fiction," Father began. "In the year 1877 among the great numbers who sought a fortune in the Black Hills was a man, whom we will know as Seals, accompanied by his wife who was stylish and handsome and his beautiful little daughter three or four years old. Seals was a newspaper man, a versatile and interesting writer, a genial, companionable fellow, given to indulgence at times to excess in the flowing bowl. He was regarded as a harmless, peaceable man in whom there were apparently none of the wreckless characteristics that would make possible the tragic events of his life.

"He settled with his little family in a quiet home in Deadwood and to the outside world peace and contentment reigned. Seals came from the state of Nevada where a few years before the sad story of his life began. He had there a particular friend and chum, and unfortunately they both fell in love with the same girl. And with a strange inconstancy she promised to marry both of them and consequently they were both happy but neither intrusted to the other the secret of his engagement. They alternated in their calls on the charmer and in escorting her to dances, parties, and entertainments of various kinds. At length these guileless suitors began to show signs of impatience and to insist upon having a day fixed for the wedding.

"When finally the young lady found it impossible to longer practice her duplicity on these unsuspecting rivals, she told them that as she could not make up her mind which of the two she would marry they must go out and settle the matter by wager of battle.

"They gallantly complied with the cruel mandate. Each took his Winchester and without second or surgeon, repaired to a lonely spot, took their positions back to back, each strode away ten paces, wheeled, and fired.

The Stagecoach Aristocracy

"Seals' rival fell severely wounded and Seals left him on the field for dead, hastened back to his heartless fiancée, and they were immediately married. The rival was not dead, but disappeared.

"Some months after Seals had taken up his residence in Deadwood he returned home late one evening to find, comfortably seated in pleasant conversation with his wife, the supposed dead rival who said to Seals as he entered: 'Well, I cannot live without her and I have come for her, so we shall have to fight that duel over again.' The challenge was instantly accepted by Seals, and with their guns they left the house.

"The next morning a stranger was found on the banks of Gold Run, near Deadwood, dead with a bullet hole in the back of his head. The body was removed to the rooms of the city undertaker who after a careful examination said he was 'the strangest bird that ever came to his joint,' for on the body he could find neither purse nor script, not even a scrap of paper by which he could be identified. Many citizens were called in to examine the stiff but no one ever had seen him while living. Seals was among the number. He seemed one of the most indifferent of the spectators, even turned the head over and examined the wound and without showing the least feeling or agitation whatever, informed the undertaker that he did not know the man, had never seen him before.

"So the stranger was laid away in a pauper's pine coffin in the potter's field. Soon thereafter, the wife and child quietly took their departure for parts un-

Old Deadwood Days

known and in a few months Seals disappeared and the incident was forgotten.

"Several years thereafter, in a distant mining camp, Seals related all the facts to a friend who had known him in the Hills, but claimed that he killed his rival in a fair duel fought on a beautiful moonlight night with no eye to see but the moon and stars, and no ear to hear but the singing rivulet. In a few days after making this statement Seals died.

"Yes," Father nodded across the table at Colonel Thornby who had started to speak. "Yes, I know, Thornby. It will be hard for anyone to conclude that the stranger was killed in a fair duel, as the wound was in the back of the head, clearly indicating foul play."

It was at Mrs. McPherson's dinner table one winter night that Mr. Remer told his story of the peerless prince of liars. The man's name was Bremen and he had been working in one of the little mines up in the mountains when Mr. Remer was with the Father DeSmet.

"All the boys from Bald Mountain and Carbonate and those camps used to come into the DeSmet office when they came down the gulch on pay day," he said. "They sat around the stove with us and talked and smoked, and when they started back to the mine, we gave them all the magazines and newspapers we were through with. We all had lots of time to read. This man Bremen was a quiet, nice sort of chap and was particularly fond of reading. Magazines and newspapers were not enough for him. He liked books and I lent him what I had. He wasn't much of a conversationalist, but he talked more to

The Stagecoach Aristocracy

me when we were alone than he did when the other boys were around. One cold night we sat alone together hugging the stove. I was reading a New York paper several weeks old that had just come in, and he had an old magazine. Something about a picture of some fellow being decorated with the Victoria Cross by the Queen of England, attracted my attention, and I showed it to Bremen. We talked about it a little and then he said quietly: 'I have one of those.' Naturally I expressed surprise. I supposed a man who had a Victoria Cross let it be known in some way. It's too great an honor to be kept in a dark corner or packed down in the bottom of a trunk.

" 'Oh, no,' he said, 'I don't care much about it. Of course my children back in the states value the cross, but I haven't much interest in it.'

" 'But what did you ever do to get a Victoria Cross?' He didn't look like a man who had lived his life in ways and places conducive to such honors. You know they don't lie around in shafts and tunnels of mines.

"He said he had been down on the Isthmus of Panama once a good many years ago when an English man-o'-war drifted into harbor with crew and passengers down with cholera. He discovered that when he and another fellow went out in a small boat to answer their distress signals. The other fellow went back with the boat but Bremen took the cholera ship to Havana. Oh, yes, he said he knew a little about navigation.

"And that is only the prelude. I supposed he did have a Victoria Cross, and was modest about it. I

believed what he said for a long time. Next pay-
day, when Bremen found me alone in the office, he
asked if I had a copy of Stanley's 'In Darkest
Africa.' I didn't have but I thought one of the
other boys had and I could borrow it for him. He
asked me not to say anything about getting it for
him because, he explained, the other fellows up at
the mine would want to read it, and he didn't like
lending borrowed books. I understood that and
promised and he went away with the book. He kept
it a good while, apologizing for it every now and
then, and in the spring he brought it back. He
thanked me and said he had enjoyed it immensely.
Early in the summer he left the Hills and I never
saw him again.

"One night in the fall some fellows who had
worked in an adjoining mine to Bremen's and lived
in a cabin close to him, were sitting around our
office fire talking, when his name was mentioned.

" 'Did you know,' one of them asked me, 'that
that fellow was in Africa with Stanley?'

" 'No!' I sat bolt upright and he went on and
untangled his story. 'Yes, it came out little by little
last spring. He didn't say much at first but finally
loosened up and told us a lot about the expedition.
You wouldn't have thought it of old Bremen, would
you? But there isn't any doubt about it because we
checked up on him. We had Stanley's book over in
our cabin and we asked him questions. He knew
all about the expedition, where they went, names of
places, and tribes and everything—things he couldn't
have known if he hadn't been there. We knew because we had the book and we checked up on him,

The Stagecoach Aristocracy

but of course we never let him know that. After he got started, he talked a lot. Stanley himself didn't know more about that expedition than Bremen did, and he threw in some little personal stuff that wasn't in the book but that fitted in so prefectly that it just made the whole thing more real. We asked him if he had read Stanley's book and he said he hadn't been able to get hold of it yet. He wanted to. So we lent him our copy then.'

"They wondered why a man like that was working in a mine at Bald Mountain. It was all right for me to look astonished. They expected me to be surprised at having a man like that among us. But I was visioning those men, one alone in his cabin with his book, his imagination and his love of vicarious adventure; the others in their cabin a stone's throw away with the same book—all reading secretly through the long winter evenings with the wind howling around and the snow drifting up to the window sills and one of them making the adventurous journey through darkest Africa real for himself and all the others.

"Bremen went to Alaska that summer and I never heard of him again, but there's a mountain of that name up there, and I wonder what wild tale he told to achieve that. Bremen isn't a common name and with his imagination, he probably could arrange some way of having it named for him."

Mrs. McPherson came down the hill across the sidewalk at the foot of her own long flight of steps, to the edge of our back-yard wall, and called to me. My bedroom window was on a level with where she stood in the bushes that had turned crimson and

Old Deadwood Days

gold. She was a dark-eyed blonde and the afternoon sunlight bringing out the bright glints in her yellow hair made her look like the friendly peaceful spirit of Indian summer. I went and sat on the window sill with my curling iron in my hand to talk to her.

"You'll have to come up and play whist to-night," she said with a little challenge in her voice. "Mrs. Hastie has just telephoned that her baby is sick and she can't come and there were only eight of us anyway."

"Oh, I hate to play whist," I objected, "and you all scold me all the time for the way I play."

"Yes," she agreed, "you play an awful game, and we'll probably scold you to-night but we'll cut the game a little short and you can redeem yourself by playing the piano. I'll expect you about eight."

Something else cut the game short sooner and more effectually than my poor game.

The McPhersons' double parlors were very cozy and charming that night. An open fire of pine logs took the autumn chill off the air that came in through the open French windows along the front of the house. Mr. McPherson was sitting with the Dagues in front of the fireplace when I came in and Mrs. McPherson called down to me from upstairs to please sit down right away and play "Annie Laurie" because Edith, the baby, was restless and that always quieted her little Scotch nerves. It was a good thing she was not a music critic because little Malcolm came and bothered me. He wanted to play a high treble obligato, and over my shoulder I was listening to the desultory talk about the near tragedy that had stalked into our own circle in the

The Stagecoach Aristocracy

afternoon. Our information was vague but appalling.

The Homestake pay train had been held up on its way out to Brownsville. The first report was that Mr. Remer, who was paymaster for the Homestake, had been killed. The contradiction followed close in its wake, with the substituted news that he and Mr. Blackstone, superintendent of the railroad, both had been seriously injured. Mr. McPherson told me when I came in that this was not true either, that no one was hurt. So far as they had been able to learn, only one of the holdup men had been wounded. They had not heard from Mr. Remer. They didn't know whether he would get down to play his hand at whist or not. But he was all right. Mr. and Mrs. Van Cise arrived just then but they had no further information. Mrs. McPherson came downstairs, the baby being pacified by our joint efforts, and we all sat around and waited. Surely Mr. Remer was coming or he would have sent word, Mrs. McPherson said, but it seemed to me that if I had been in a holdup, I easily could forget all about a whist engagement. But then it would have been easy for me under any circumstances to forget about whist.

When he came, apologetic for his lateness, his entrance was that of a star into a carefully prepared stage scene. He looked tired but there were no signs of blood or battle smoke about him and he was inclined to be reticent about his day's work. We didn't play whist. We devoted ourselves to drawing out the story of this holdup that sounded like the 'seventies and yet had thrust itself into our very

271

midst so that we almost could hear the rattle of shot, smell the powder smoke, and see the elusive masked faces in the brush on the mountain side.

Mr. Remer said he was in the engine cab with Commiskey, the engineer, and Morgan, the fireman. Mr. Blackstone was on the first of the string of flat cars they were taking out to the wood camp for timber for the mine. On another of these flat cars was the section crew that played the part of Fate in the protection of the Homestake men and money. Mr. Remer had twelve thousand dollars to pay off the men at Brownsville. It was in an old yellow valise in the tool box on the tender. Across his knees he carried an old double-barreled, sawed-off shotgun.

On the straight stretch of track in Reno Gulch, the train came almost to a stop to let the section crew off. It still was running slowly, not yet under full headway when it reached the curve leading to the trestle and ran into the spread rails. Commiskey could stop it at once instead of hurtling with it into the gulch as the men who spread the rails had planned. It would have been easy to take the money away from dead men in an overturned engine. The holdup men were so close, however, that they took a long chance. They sprang up from their brush cover on the hillside with mad yells of "Hands up. Throw up your hands, you—" and began shooting.

Return fire from the engine cab had put the robbers to rout before the arrival of help from Woodville summoned by Commiskey's long screeching engine whistle, and had won for Billy Remer

The Stagecoach Aristocracy

the sobriquet of "Buck Shot Bill." It was a wild fight while it lasted. Shots spattered into the engine cab like hail. One bullet struck the boiler head between Remer and the fireman who were standing close together, splashed, and tore out the glass in the fireman's window. The marvel was that no one of the men on the train was shot.

Mr. Remer went on out to Brownsville, paid off the men who had heard first that he was killed, then that the money was lost, and were amazed when he appeared, not only safe himself but with the pay roll intact.

"You bet your sweet life," Bill Sweeney had said, "they didn't take the money away from Buck Shot Bill."

Never before had anyone of our own wandered in straight from the thick of a train robbery and we had little consideration for his weariness. One of the holdup men who had been wounded, had been captured, he said, and brought to Deadwood while he went on to Brownsville with the pay roll. They probably would get the second wounded man who had left a trail of scattered drops of blood through the underbrush. The other two seemed to have made their escape.

Then he rose and apologized to Mrs. McPherson for his obvious fatigue. "Come, Estelline," he said. "I'll take you home."

We walked along Forest avenue—the street that had no road, only a sidewalk—down the Guy street steps to Williams street and home, talking casually about a new book he was reading and would bring to me the next time he came down, about the danc-

273

ing club that was preparing for the winter balls to be given in our various houses, and A. D. Wilson's interest in Irene. Not one word of the Homestake pay-roll holdup in which he had faced death only a few hours before. I can't remember that I ever heard him speak of it again.

The General got a good deal of pleasure out of that Homestake holdup. It proved to him that even in what he called "these decadent late 'eighties," the old West was not dead. When a man undertook to carry a pay roll, he carried it through. A little shooting-up on the side was part of the day's work to be met courageously and dismissed casually.

Deadwood's flair for dancing was deflected seriously only once. Roller skating was the furious fad of one season and then died a slow death while dancing snapped into its own again. As long as the furor lasted, nobody did anything else. We had to give time to it because it took time to learn to skate whereas no one of us could remember when we learned to dance. We skated in the opera house and in unoccupied store buildings which always were terribly transient. We skated mornings, noons, and nights. Those of us who were in school, down where the grades would have been if the schools had been graded, skated through the noon hour, after school, and in the early evenings when Father and the General came down to act as judges in races and contests. They wouldn't risk their dignity trying to learn to skate. Most of their friends and contemporaries did tumble around in little exclusive clubs where there were no experts to jeer at their lack of skill.

The Stagecoach Aristocracy

The sport attracted even the Indians for one brief visit. A group of them who were attending United States court visited the rink one night with Billy McLaughlin, their attorney, who was entertaining them. One old fellow who never had been afraid of anything in the world, from paleface soldiers to shooting fire, was persuaded to put on a pair of what he called the "little wagons." After he had fallen down several times, he gave up trying to manage them, grinned, nodded pleasantly all around, and went away.

The rink was such a gold mine that it precipitated a nice wicked little war between the owner and the lessee that was carried on in the dark of the night. Members of the Midnight Club were the only skaters who saw it in action. The city marshal came in the first time just as they were leaving and arrested all of the owner's employees who were going to make some improvements. That is—he thought he arrested them all but most of them hid in the depths of some forest scenery on the stage and when everything was quiet they stole out and took possession.

This was repeated for several nights in succession and then the owner won because the lessee hadn't paid his rent. The roller skating never stopped. Little we cared who was in possession. But I wished I could have belonged to the Midnight Club.

Melodrama enough, Mother thought, strutted over our own threshold without our going out to look for it. Unexpected guests came along strange trails into our house through the wide double front

Old Deadwood Days

doors that never were locked, and in summer, never closed.

One morning just before daylight we were roused by an alarm of fire. The hose carts were in the street in front of our house and the window panes in Mother's room when we all hurried to see where the fire was, were too hot to touch. The whole world was red from the high-flung blaze. The flimsy old frame houses of Main street were burning like pitch pine in a bonfire and from directly under the hill below us, Belle Haskell's house, "The 400," was a wild crimson flame. Men and women in all sorts of disarray were scrambling up the hillside, firemen were shouting orders, and our neighbors from higher, safer ground were ringing our bell and calling us to get dressed and pack up.

Father was out of town which Mother and the General agreed was not a bad thing. He would have had us all up on the top of the mountain with everything we owned. The General thought it would be safe to wait a few minutes before carrying out the piano and the kitchen range. Robbie had gone over the hill to the log stable where he kept his donkey to see if it were safe. Gaylord and Francis Babcock in hot haste dragged the hose cart out of the little hose house up opposite the Babcocks' only to find when they arrived at the hydrant nearest the fire that their hose had no nozzle and couldn't be attached.

Our danger passed in a very short time and because we were so close to the fire line, women began to congregate with Mother in our kitchen to make coffee and sandwiches for the firemen. Mrs.

The Stagecoach Aristocracy

McConnell and Mrs. Cheairs, and Mrs. McPherson were there, and I don't know how many more. Halle and Lenore McConnell and I were kept busy serving firemen, and carrying coffee out to those who couldn't find time to come in.

It was Lenore who discovered, in the very hottest of the turmoil, a woman lying on a mattress in the middle of the street where the firemen had laid her out of the way of the fire when they carried her out of "The 400."

"Dear me," said Lenore standing over her in great concern, "she'll get pneumonia."

"She's got it already," grieved a half-dressed man beside them. "She'll die now."

It was not the way of a McConnell to see a catastrophe coming and not try to prevent it. Lenore hurried in to the house talking to Halle and me as she went, and we brought Mother back with us.

"Bring her into the house immediately," Mother commanded the firemen nearest her. They were all volunteers and she knew them—had known most of them since their kilt days. "She never should have been left here at all. What were you thinking of? I'll make a place in the living room."

The young men stood there perfectly still for a moment.

"Into your house, Mrs. Bennett?" one of them asked with amazed emphasis on the pronoun.

Without stopping on her way, Mother cast him a look that should have put out the fire. "Yes," she said, "into my house."

They picked up the mattress and following on Mother's heels, carried the sick woman into our

277

living room, where Mrs. McConnell looked after her while Mother sent Gaylord and Francis after Dr. Babcock. The woman didn't die.

The fire had settled down into a heavy flame-shot smoke when Halle discovered two girls sitting forlornly on a little trunk near the edge of the hill. We told Mother about them, too. We thought they hadn't had any breakfast, and she went out and asked them to come in. Halle and I waited on them and then sat down and talked to them while they drank their coffee and ate their sandwiches. Most of the crowd had been fed by that time. They told us about the fire, how it had broken out just after they had gone to bed. They didn't know how it happened. It had not started in their house. They told us their names but that was all they told us about themselves. I don't remember their last names. Kitty was a dimpled little girl with short curly brown hair and a saucy nose. She seemed to like life just as it was. Mabel was tall and slender with serious eyes. She walked over to the window when she had finished breakfast—the window that looked out through the red-berried branches of the rowan tree to the wide expanse of fire devastated town.

"You've no idea," she said without looking around, "what it means to girls like us to have a woman like your mother ask us into her house. You'll never know." They thanked us cordially and quietly went away.

The next day Halle met Mabel in Liebmann's dry goods store and spoke to her.

"She seemed surprised," Halle said when she was

The Stagecoach Aristocracy

telling Mother and me about it. "She didn't think I would speak to her."

"It won't hurt you at all," Mother said. "I would be sorry if you hadn't spoken to her."

The next we heard of Mabel was a story in the *Pioneer*. She had committed suicide by taking laudanum. She left no note nor explanation. She had told no one of any such thought. One of the girls knew about her people and how to reach them. She came from a respectable family living on a ranch near Custer.

Mother and Mrs. McConnell went with Mr. McConnell to meet the father and mother when they came up to take their daughter home. They told the mother that they had known Mabel through their daughters and in some miraculous way kept from her the facts that would have made her grief more cruel.

Noblesse oblige!

When the Railroad Came

Chapter 10

WHEN THE RAILROAD CAME

WITH a flash of glory and blazoning of heroic achievement the first railroad train swept triumphantly into Deadwood one December morning just as the sun shot a brilliant salutation through a cloud that had been hanging over the shimmering head of White Rocks.

It rushed into a tempestuous welcome that had been waiting fifteen years. It closed the old stage-coach days that had run their little span of pioneer life parallel with the hostile Indian.

The first stagecoach dashed into Deadwood the year that Custer and his command were massacred on the Little Big Horn. The first railroad train roared in on the day the Sioux nation laid down its arms at the battle of Wounded Knee.

A long picturesque adventurous chapter in the winning of the West was closed on December 29, 1890. A new day dawned with that burst of sunlight over White Rocks, that strange new rush of power into the gulch, and the last homeward march from the reservation of the Seventh Cavalry—Custer's old regiment.

That was the wildest fall and early winter I can remember—the closing of the last of the stagecoach years. The Chicago and Northwestern, the pioneer railway of South Dakota that had been scouting along the old Indian and stagecoach trails since it started north from Chadron, was less than ten miles away. The dirt was flying ahead of the track-layers, and we could hear the dynamite explosions in the running of the tunnel.

Disturbing rumors of Indians on the warpath had been coming into Deadwood all through the fall. Every night when the sob of a pine tree just outside my window seemed to change into a weird war whoop for a startled moment before it died down into the little crooning song again, I had to reassure myself with the thought of Fort Meade, unslumbering and serene, a scant fifteen miles away on the road to the reservations. I remembered always through the dark night quiet that might be shattered any moment, the conversation that had taken place at our dinner table once several years before when the question of abandoning the post was under consideration.

"If they abolish Fort Meade," Father had said to Dakota's delegate to Congress who was our guest, "there will be nothing between us and the Sioux."

A serious gravity in his face and voice told tomes of what might happen if there was nothing between us and the Sioux. It was the only time I ever heard him suggest that the Indians might be a menace. It was part of his policy of dealing with his children never to give us a hint of alarm. We were surrounded by so much danger he could not let us be afraid. He gave me then a new thought about the cavalry post where Custer's old regiment was stationed and where Comanche, the white horse that had been found on that bloody battlefield—the only thing alive—had been kept in government authorized luxury until he died of old age. Fort Meade became all at once something more than a well ordered symmetrical picture, a place where we went to dance and to watch the cavalry drill. It was the effective guardian of the Hills.

There was comfort in knowing it was there, yet in the midst of so much alarm in that unquiet fall of 1890, I wondered a good deal if Fort Meade and its cavalry would prove adequate against all the hostile tribes between the Missouri River and the Big Horn Mountains.

According to word from Hermosa, about one hundred and fifty Indians with their families were camped on Battle Creek close by. They claimed to be friendly but the people in and around Hermosa were badly frightened and ranchers and settlers were coming into town for protection. The same news came from all the valley towns. People were hurrying to safety. Those who lived nearest the towns were driving their stock with them—those who came from long distances left everything behind that they might make the most possible speed. News from Pine Ridge and Rosebud agencies was not reassuring.

Late in November one of Charley Fargo's wood haulers brought word of having seen Indians riding furtively through the woods close to Deadwood. In December hostile Indians were destroying United States Army camps and moving toward Pine Ridge.

All the time the railroad was coming closer mile by mile. Frequently the hobos at work on the grade

Old Deadwood Days

came into Deadwood and got drunk, raising a terrific disturbance. It is something I am sure would have been noticed even in '76. The General said it was different.

One day in December a lone hobo came in and made a loud noise about enlisting three hundred men to go down and fight under General Miles, but he got drunk almost immediately and forgot his mission.

Late one afternoon a hobo whose name was Tony Newbar, according to the police reports of the next day, came up on Forest Hill with a couple of friends. He left them standing on the sidewalk while he came up to our house and rang the bell. When I opened the front door he swore a string of oaths and quickly rejoined his companions. All three of them stood there shouting at me language I didn't understand. It was their idea of a pleasant time. I slammed the door and called Father on the telephone. They repeated their little amusement at the Cloughs and Wringroses before he reached Williams street with a policeman who took them in charge. Father came on home, the maddest man who ever walked a Deadwood street.

One holiday—I don't remember whether it was Thanksgiving or Christmas—the hoboes invaded the town in such numbers and with such drunken disregard for the peace of the town that the police finally cornered them in Wall street, where they were defying all law and authority, and turned the fire hose on them. We sat in our bay window and watched it—a short rough melodrama. Not very nice, but exciting.

When the Railroad Came

Small wonder that the French and English newspapers that fall thought: "Deadwood, Dakota, U.S.A., was having considerable trouble with the Hobo Indians."

The last stagecoach rolled out of Deadwood Sunday afternoon like a grand old actor taking his final curtain. Its escort of Knights of Pythias was in plain clothes and carried canes instead of swords, and the band played a little plaintively, "Fare thee well, for I must leave thee." But Frank Hunter, the last of the stage drivers, gathered his ribbons up over the six white horses and flourished his whip, and the horses curved their necks and pranced a little in starting as though the railroad still was two hundred miles away. Their game was closed but they were good losers.

The next morning the horses, munching their oats in the stable at Whitewood, heard the familiar whistle of the incoming train and pricked up their ears in surprise. They should have been at the station in their nickel plated harness to carry on to Deadwood when the train stopped. But everything was quiet around the stables. No stock tenders, no drivers interrupted their oats. There was more noise and confusion than usual and then the train went on, the sound of its heavy breathing growing less as it was lost in the mountains, and the horses were left behind.

In those twenty-two hours of a closing year, between the last stagecoach and the first train, the most typical mining camp of the West was changed into a distributing center between the mines and the railroad. The essential qualities that made Deadwood a flaming frontier town went out with the old stage-coach or were ground to dust under the wheels of the incoming railroad train.

The little prelude to the railroad was the narrow gauge Deadwood Central that ran between Deadwood and Lead for less than two years before the coming of the real railroad from the outlands. It had a good deal of trouble getting itself built. For one thing, its right of way was more like a ladder than a roadbed. It sprang from one town to the other and in so doing got into trouble with the mountain side and the toll gates. Gold Run is a narrow gulch and while the wagon road ran along on its side of the creek in comparative security, the railroad seemed to have stirred up the whole mountain. It acted like an outraged giant flinging great masses of rock down on the grade and interfering seriously with the building of the road. The Gold Run toll road that was crossed five times by the D. C. right of way, stopped it twice and took it into court claiming that in cutting out the hill and loosening the rock, the railroad was making the toll road dangerous. When it was the railroad that had had all the trouble with the loose-acting rock. But the railroad won and continued its climb. The toll road was near the end of its usefulness anyway. It belonged to a day that was passing.

The Deadwood Central achieved an immediate and spectacular popularity. Deadwood and Lead people traveled back and forth for the pleasure and the novelty of the traveling. In the days of hacks and bad roads we went when it was necessary and grumbled.

When the Railroad Came

Wing Tsue, the Chinese merchant, took his three small children up on the first train and they were so enchanted with the journey that they insisted upon going every day. Whereupon he detailed an old Chinaman to take them back and forth until they tired of the sport, but that wasn't for weeks.

"Little Betsy," a baby locomotive that smiled and dimpled over all the fuss and attention she received, was the first locomotive Deadwood ever saw. She wasn't much bigger than a good sized nugget from Potato Gulch and with her bulging smokestack she looked like a cute, saucy little girl wearing a coal scuttle over her head to play lady. The next engine that ran on the Deadwood Central when business got too heavy for Betsy to handle alone, was a gaunt sort of thing they called "Sitting Bull" because she was "a bad injun." I think they got her second-hand some place. Never was there another like Betsy, but I did not realize fully the lovable charm of her until the high moment when I sat in the engineer's seat and pulled a lever in response to which little Betsy moved slowly out of the Deadwood station. She throbbed and moved like a lovely baby giantess unconscious of her power, and, trailing obediently along behind, came her train of two cars. The engineer stood close beside me and directed the driving, but it was my hand that moved the engine. I felt as though I were directing the movements of planetary systems.

People who never have run a locomotive have missed, I am sure, the supreme sensation of power. An automobile goes all at once—not gaining momentum smoothly and majestically like a locomo-

Old Deadwood Days

tive, and it has no retinue of cars following its curves, its *accelerandos,* and *retardandos.* Even an airplane flies alone, but a locomotive always has a following.

I stopped several rods short of the platform at Lead, but I managed to get under way again and stop somewhere near the right place. I noticed the alighting passengers looked curiously at the engine, but they were of no importance. They were mere people who rode in cars that Betsy and I controlled.

They wouldn't let me run her back to Deadwood. It seems it requires more skill and quicker judgment to drive an engine down grade than up—which is not true of everything. From that day I felt that Betsy and I had been on a high adventure among the stars.

After that I could not have allowed anyone else to carry her banner in the carnival. The Merchants' Carnival was given by the women of the Congregational Church to raise money. Their need could be counted on for at least one important social function a season, to say nothing of numberless smaller ones. Business men paid a stipulated sum to be represented in the carnival by young women and girls who were costumed to advertise the firms. Mother, Mrs. Cushman, Mrs. Mather, and Mrs. L. C. Miller were in charge, but I don't know how they could have done it without Irene and me. We did nothing, it seemed, for weeks but run around to see business men. We helped design costumes, and we rehearsed. We were so busy we almost forgot about the incoming Chicago and Northwestern Railroad, and the threatening Indian troubles.

When the Railroad Came

The day before the carnival word came to Deadwood of the killing of two cowboys and six soldiers by the Indians. There was a rumor that Noah Newbank, a freighter, had been killed by the Sioux while crossing the reservation from Pierre. The news from the Pine Ridge reservation was increasingly alarming, and settlers were continuing to flock into Rapid City, forty miles away in the foothills.

On Friday, the day of the carnival, the thermometer dropped to ten degrees below zero. But nothing interfered with the gayety.

There was a grand march of nearly forty of these living advertisements around the hall, all of us carrying banners to explain ourselves. At the end of the grand march we lined up in double column, stepped forward and saluted when our firm names were read, and for each one Father read a verse that he and the General and Mr. Van Cise and Mr. McConnell had written.

Irene represented the Merchants National Bank and wore a pink surah silk gown with high-powered bills all over it. She looked as though she owned the United States treasury and the mint too. Her embroidered pink crêpe shawl that her China boy —meaning the one she used to teach in Chinese school—had given her, didn't make her look any less affluent. You hardly could count the bills on her and we didn't have any paper dollars out there either.

Lenore was the Keystone Hotel and all a-jangle with knives, forks, and spoons. Her banner was in the shape of a waiter's tray and was surmounted by a big tin coffee pot.

Old Deadwood Days

Emily Wringrose in a white satin gown so shining with ornaments it might as well have been alpaca, was a marching jewelry store and at the same time a walking page of history because the Black Hills jewelry she wore is a visualized story of gold mining and gold manufacture in the West. Mr. Butler, whose father was one of those who brought the design to Deadwood, told me about it and if it had not been for my railroad I would have envied Emily.

Mr. Butler said the little cluster of gold grape leaves with their occasional tiny bunch of grapes marked the trail of the gold miner. Wherever gold is manufactured into jewelry in the same camp in which it is mined the little gold grape design appears. No place else. The golden legend trailed its way from the California of '49 to Deadwood, the last of the old-time gold camps where it stopped and became a permanent and distinctive product. The design first was made in the early days of the gold excitement in California by jewelers who had crossed the plains in emigrant wagons. It was a craft appreciation of the wonder of seeing abundant growing grapes in the Sacramento Valley after their long months on the plains. True to the traditions of their trade they chose their design from the most attractive natural model at hand. The single grape leaf had been used in decorations, Mr. Butler said, but the clustered leaves and fruit of the golden state jewelers was entirely their own. They followed the prospectors from California to Colorado, Montana, and the Black Hills and wherever the gold came into their hands direct from placer

When the Railroad Came

streams and quartz veins, they made it up in the little grape leaf design.

Halle hadn't been paying much attention to the carnival so that when it was brought to Mother's notice that Job Lawrenson who with his partner, Colonel Bogey, owned the livery stable at the foot of the Gold street steps, hadn't been able to get anyone to represent him and therefore probably couldn't be in the carnival and contribute his money to the Congregational deficit, Mother thought of Halle with a faint hope. A faint and remote hope it was. She had no reason to think her young daughter would be different from the other girls, who all refused to be livery stables. She approached her with unwonted meekness. But Halle always was surprising her. This time she was prompt and cheerful in her willingness to be anything at all anyone—especially Mother—wanted her to be. She tumbled over backward in volunteering to be the "Bucket o' Blood" saloon, a Chinese laundry, or the Whoop-up corral where she'd have to have yokes of oxen bellowing along with her in the grand march. In fact, she rather fancied that idea of bellowing oxen. It would be unique and would attract attention. She was full of ideas and terribly amiable.

Mr. Lawrenson promised her the "finest costume in the carnival." And she had it. The rest of us furnished ours as best we could. She had a heavy white satin gown with a red silk horse net draped over it, a little red and white jockey cap, a long carriage whip, and a banner with a prancing steed done in oils.

The dark serge frock I wore had a railroad track

that my mother constructed from gold and silver braid, running around the bottom of the skirt. I had a little coat with brass buttons down the front, and I had borrowed the day conductor's cap and punch and red lantern. Gaylord says he subtracted several cubits from his stature that day the way he had to run around the railroad yards assembling my costume. On my white satin, gold-fringed banner was painted a portrait of my little friend Betsy.

A few days after the carnival Father told me one night at dinner that Mr. Coe, president of the Deadwood Central, wanted to see me. Would I come into his office the next time I was down town? I went the next morning. No railroad president ever had sent for me before and I was too curious to wait. His office was in the corner of the Syndicate block overlooking Red Creek. From the window we could see, across the bridge and down the length of Lee street, the tracks of the D. C. with Betsy standing, fretting at the bit, ready to go to Lead.

Mr. Coe whom I knew pretty well in private life but who seemed an entirely different person in his high official life, told me very seriously and impressively that the company was so well pleased with its representation at the merchant's carnival that they were offering me an annual pass over the road. He took my breath away. Naturally, considering my very limited experience with railways, I had none at all with passes. I felt as though I had been offered a magic carpet to tour the world with a side excursion through the planets. That pass opened up a vista of worlds like a great telescope. What matter that it could carry me no farther than Lead,

When the Railroad Came

less than four miles up Gold Run, where I had been a thousand times? It roused in me a sudden and irresistible wanderlust, and it spanned for me the gulf between the stagecoach days I loved and the new railroad ways I didn't know.

It was a dark cold Monday morning that found us all assembled in the narrow north end of Deadwood Gulch to meet the fist through train from Chicago. We gathered early on the scant platform of the little station that later grew into a freight depot. Deadwood in December is dark at eight o'clock in the morning. There was not a glint of light on the pinnacle of White Rocks rising high above the town on the east. But people were everywhere. They crowded the platform. They lined the uneven board sidewalks and filled the rough frozen street. They covered the house tops and clambered up the side of the hill on the west. No inch of room anywhere that could command a view of the waiting track's new shining rails, but was crammed with crowds—a heterogeneous, hilarious multitude, some of whom never had seen a railroad train before. They came from Lead, Central City, Terraville, Spearfish—places that knew nothing of railroads; and from the train-wise towns of Chadron, Rapid City, and Whitewood. They came in carriages, on horseback, and on foot. The entire population of the northern Hills was there.

Deadwood, from the southernmost house of Cleveland by the green houses, to the northern end of Fountain City was in a gala array that no Fourth of July or Pioneer Day ever had evoked. Flags were flung from every building and banners across every

Old Deadwood Days

street. The Deadwood and Terraville bands marched down the gulch with merry music and fine uniforms. The volunteer fire departments called a complete roster. The Homestake hose company pulled its shining nickel-plated cart that it called a "hose carriage," and carried a hand-painted satin banner. The Hook-and-Ladder and South Deadwood hose companies dragged all their fire equipment and flaunted gorgeous silken standards. The Uniform Rank Knights of Pythias turned out their drill corps with full quota in splendid glittering uniforms. Everything Deadwood and the up-gulch towns could muster contributed color, music, and gayety. At intervals from somewhere up on the hill came heavy welcoming explosions of giant powder.

Mother, Mrs. Cushman, Mrs. Mather and some other women I don't remember had chairs at the windows in the station. Robbie and some other small boys had a vantage point on a strange looking thing they said was a baggage truck. Halle and Madge and Floy Bullock—Floy the most beautiful thing even in the trying morning dusk, that ever grew up in Deadwood—were trying to cheer up the General and Captain Bullock who had been a little low in spirit ever since the stagecoach went out the day before. Papa was standing talking to Colonel Steele and Gaylord was close beside him, never moving, never taking his eyes from the point of expectation. He never had seen a railroad train.

We had been waiting ever since I could remember for this coming train, yet the short hour on the station platform in spite of all the excitement, seemed a long expectant day. Every now and then

When the Railroad Came

some one connected with the railroad would come out of the station to encourage us and tell us the train would be here now in a few moments, and one of the bands would strike up blithely: "Will you come? Will you come? O, you never will regret it if you come." Mrs. Cheairs called down the length of the platform to the Northwestern agent in Deadwood: "I'll bet you ten dollars, Mr. Harmon, that it doesn't get in till next year." The band played snatches from "Patience."

Mike Heffron and another man, waiting patiently like the rest of us, were standing right behind me where I balanced perilously on the train-side edge of the platform, one hand in Billy Remer's overcoat pocket for warmth and security. Irene, on the other side of me was sure I was going to have the distinction of being the first victim of a railroad accident in Deadwood.

"Well, Mike," said the man I didn't know, "you can spend your pile now. Here's your chance."

"How?" Mike asked with interest.

His friend had time to recall the story while we waited. "Don't you remember that hard winter of '76 and '77?"

Sure, Mike had not forgotten. "An' don't you remember one night we were all sitting around in Col. Thompson's cabin down where the Homestake stamp mills are now, around that big old fireplace of his on stools and empty boxes?"

Mike could recall a lot of nights like that.

"Well, this was a mighty stormy night and mighty cold but we had plenty of wood and we all had forty-dollar ore in our claims, and had the world

Old Deadwood Days

by the tail, generally. We were all telling what we were going to do when we sold our mines. You were wrapped up in a California blanket up in a bunk, smoking your pipe and not paying much attention till somebody called to you and asked you: 'Mike, what are you going to do when you make your raise?' An' you took your pipe out of your mouth slow like and said, 'Boys, when I make my raise I'm going to ride out in a Pullman palace car.' An' we all laughed at you. We'd just heard that a man named Pullman had invented a car that people could undress and go to bed in and sleep comfortably while they traveled along. Don't you remember? We none of us ever expected to see one, but they tell me there's one coming in with this train an' I reckon you've got the price of a ticket on it."

"Sure," said Mike Heffron, "I'll go out to-night just to show you. I'll go to wherever it is at breakfast time, in that sleeping car bed so's to stay all night."

They tell me that pioneer train arrived promptly according to schedule at 8:45 A.M. on Monday morning, December 29, 1890, while Mayor Star called a truce in his war on the gamblers, and Col. Forsyth and his Seventh Cavalry brought the long Sioux war to an end. But as I remember it, we waited hours in the sharp dusky morning, hours that we counted as nothing against the years.

Suddenly from the black mouth of the tunnel a spiral of smoke swirled up and was lost in the splash of sunlight on White Rocks' limestone peak. Some one shouted "She's coming." The band struck up, "O, say, can you see by the dawn's early light?"

When the Railroad Came

Men's hats came off and the world of Deadwood Gulch stood at attention. The train came all at once. There was no watching it approach as in a valley or prairie country. It strained and thundered triumphantly up the grade into a shouting tumult that frightened a grizzly bear in his winter quarters at Ragged Top, reverberated up and down the gulch and around the head of Terry's Peak, startled an old prospector who in his remote cabin on French Creek, did not know what was happening, and scattered out into the blue snowy valleys. People added their wild huzzas to the blare of the brass bands and the dynamite explosions. A cordial whistle from a new and optimistic reduction plant shrieked a welcome and the locomotive whistle answered.

The train came up beside the platform panting and heaving just as the six white stage horses had done the day before. But the train had come from Chicago in less time than it had taken the stagecoach to cross the old Sioux reservation from the Missouri River. It brought with it the speed, the luxury, and the easy contacts of the closing century. It brought the "effete East" to our very doorsteps. It closed the era that had made Deadwood famous.

The shouting and acclaim died out as the officers of the Deadwood Club ushered the railway officials into carriages and took them to the club for luncheon. The band led the way playing "Hail, the conquering hero comes." The rest of us walked up in the wake of the diminuendo strains that changed wistfully to, "Back to your mountain home."

That had come about for which Deadwood had been working and hoping for nearly fifteen years.

Old Deadwood Days

It was a dream come true, a whole shaft-full of hopes realized, but it had plunged us—people of the mountains and gulches and stagecoaches—into a new order of things that we didn't quite understand. It was something like being told, "You're not a little girl any more. You are grown up. You can't walk stilts or play hop-scotch in the street. You mustn't dance on the sidewalk to the music of the Gem Theater band, and you should give your dolls to your little sister." It is a fine thing to grow up and realize your ambitions but there is a little wrench about it that tugs at your heart for a moment.

That night at dinner after he had said grace, Father looked around the table at our lifted faces still flushed and bright eyed from the excitement of the morning. "Well," he said, "we'll have to lock our doors now."

The End